We've never done it like this before.

10 creative approaches to the same old church tasks

C. JEFF WOODS

An Alban Institute Publication

The Publications Program of The Alban Institute is assisted by a grant from Trinity Church, New York City.

Library of Congress Catalog Card Number 93-74584
ISBN 1-56699-124-2

CONTENTS

88374

ACKNOWLEDGMENTS

I thank God for the care I receive each day and the guidance to perform the ministries to which I have been called. I appreciate the wonderful gift of the Holy Spirit.

I thank God for my family. My wife, Kandy, is a great encourager. My children, Brandon and Kelsey, are a constant joy. My parents provided a home where ministry was as commonplace as eating.

I also thank God for others who have been an inspiration to me. Dr. Harold H. Harty served as my mentor in my "fascination years" with the field of organizational theory. He served as an excellent role model, providing balanced support and challenge as I pursued the field with rigor. The classes of Dr. David Clark not only introduced me to nonorthodox organizational theories, but also taught me to apply them to the real world. I am indebted to Jane Cumberworth for reviewing the manuscript and giving many helpful suggestions, and to Celia Hahn and Evelyn Bence for their editing. I am grateful to Jan Wojcik, my college composition professor, whose plethoretic red marks taught me much about writing. Larry Sayre and Mike Hankins offered me the opportunity to conduct leacdership workshops. The discussions from those workshops became background material for this manuscript. Finally, the members of First Baptist Church of Rushville, Indiana, are a great inspiration as they serve as my partners in ministry.

INTRODUCTION

Church leaders often follow "tradition." For some that means continuing the same bureaucratic organizational patterns that have endured
since the beginning of this century. Yet the bureaucratic model, developed by Max Weber as he analyzed the hierarchy of the ancient Catholic
Church and the military system, is seldom helpful for churches today.
Church leaders need a new way to lead.

This book will introduce the reader to ten new ways to lead in
the church. Although the ten theories presented are diverse, they have
something in common. Each challenges a basic assumption about organizing. Within each chapter, I will draw attention to and challenge
one widely held assumption.

Nonorthodox organizational theorists are working to break down
the dominant paradigm in organizational theory because the dominant
paradigm is failing to show how organizations truly function in today's
world. These nonorthodox theories provide an alternative viewpoint of
today's organizations.

The dominant paradigm of today is still the bureaucratic model.
The bureaucratic model claims to operate in an efficient, predictable, and
rational way. Even when we discover that organizations are no longer
operating in this manner (if they ever did), it is scary to announce that
we are about to adopt a new viewpoint, one that views organizations as
inefficient, unpredictable, and irrational! As the reader can easily see,
along the way we will need to develop new language for our new paradigm of organizing.

The presentation of each theory begins with a scenario within a
local church setting. Each chapter contains six sections: (1) the scenario,
(2) options, (3) the theory, (4) past application, (5) future application,

and (6) how to use this chapter with a small group. The scenarios trace the leader development of a hypothetical character named Phoebe. Phoebe is first given the task of editing a Christmas devotional guide for her church. As Phoebe contemplates the various options suggested by three of her friends, she runs into a professor from her college days who teaches organizational theory. The professor, Dr. Harold Hastings, assists Phoebe with her options. Dr. Hastings's role is similar to the "good neighbor" character in ABC's "Home Improvement" show.

Dr. Hastings's advice proves very beneficial. As Phoebe performs each new assignment with some degree of success, she is naturally asked to take on more and more responsibility, eventually becoming a member of the diaconate. Others in Phoebe's church, including her pastor and minister of Christian education, hear of Dr. Hastings and ask for Phoebe's permission to contact him with their own dilemmas. As each scenario unfolds, Phoebe and others in her church continue to seek the help and resources of Dr. Hastings.

Each scenario in which Phoebe and her friends become involved is a type of dilemma. The theory presented in each chapter shows a way to think about problems and their solutions. The theories are easily adapted to new situations, and readers are encouraged to make new applications of the theories in their local congregations.

While I have tried to create a sense of flow from chapter to chapter, it is not critical that the chapters be read or discussed in the order presented. While the book could easily be read within one sitting, it might be easier to absorb it in sections or chapter by chapter. The last section of each chapter presents suggestions for group study. Some of these sections expound upon information already presented in the chapter and others present new methods of digesting the material.

The book is intended for both clergy and laity. In our changing world, church leaders must look for new ways to lead. We must also begin breaking down the barriers between professional church leaders and laity and learn to lead together.

CHAPTER I

The GAS Theory:
Looking for Complete Solutions

The Scenario

Phoebe loved Christmas—despite the stress of the season. And stress there was. Although very little battery resulted from her efforts, Phoebe assaulted the season, not wanting to miss anything Christmas had to offer. In December every room of Phoebe's house announced Christmas to her guests. The food, the music, the decorations, and the atmosphere all carried a festive flavor. Besides the traditional shopping and wrapping, Phoebe reached out to those who would not have full holiday calendars. Phoebe visited in the nursing home, baked goods for the homebound, and always took more than one tag from the gift list tree at the Salvation Army.

One afternoon in early November Phoebe was preparing dinner with her youngest daughter. They were rehearsing appropriate and inappropriate replies to Grandmother's "And what would Elizabeth like for Christmas this year?" question. The phone intruded—the pastor calling, proceeding with the usual greeting, then switching to something radically unexpected.

"Would you be willing to organize a Christmas devotional guide this year? Instead of purchasing a published resource, I thought we might tap the resources of our own members."

Phoebe took a deep breath as the pastor continued, "We would need the devotionals to the church secretary by November 25—to have them ready for the Hanging of the Greens Service on the twenty-ninth."

"You know I'm not an organizer," Phoebe countered.

"I know you have told me that before, and I will respect your decision if you choose not to do the task, but . . . " (Phoebe knew the clincher was coming) " . . . I thought of you because of your deep sense of compassion for others at this time of the year. If you accept, I know you are the type to give this project the attention it needs. Why don't you think and pray about it for a couple of days? Then let me know."

"Okay," Phoebe said, somewhat unwillingly. Who could argue with the pastor about praying over an issue for a couple of days?

Phoebe's anxiety stemmed from her fear of organizing rather than from disapproval of the project. Although administration, leadership, and organizing always enticed Phoebe, she was not a born organizer as were many in the congregation. *Why didn't the pastor give this project to someone else?* was her first and lingering thought on the matter.

Options

Like many people Phoebe felt obliged to accept a position in the church simply because she was asked. Unfortunately, the task offered no job description. Phoebe's pastor, Mark, never considered himself an administrator. "I'm more of a people person than a task person," he would tell others. Over the years Mark had been wise enough to involve others in administrative assignments. And now Phoebe had two days in which to decide whether or not to accept the assignment.

Mark was not a person who was afraid to implement new ideas. When faced with implementing a yearly program, Mark often looked for a new approach to appeal to the changing climate of his congregation. Mark believed that while tradition is always a reason for celebration, it should never be a reason for administration. But neither was Mark a person who developed very many new ideas himself. He depended a great deal upon the creativity of others like Phoebe.

Many churches today are looking for new ways to do things, new ways to lead, new ways to accomplish old tasks. Many authors have suggested that the church is experiencing a paradigm shift. The environment of the church and church members themselves are changing. Jude Dougherty suggests,

> The recent shift . . . from a dominant Protestant to a secular
> outlook has created a new set of problems. The Catholic Church

is no longer faced with the task of defending Catholicism against Protestantism, but of defending Christianity itself in the face of major attack.[1]

For many reasons the church is being forced to discover a whole new way of being the church in today's world. To keep up with the changes in people's lives, the church will need to attempt some new methods. Phoebe, Mark, and other leaders in her church are about to embark upon a journey of learning new ways to lead in the church.

On the evening following the conversation with her pastor, Phoebe attended a church cell group meeting at Sarah's home. Following the meeting, Phoebe told Jim, Larry, and other members of the cell group good-bye and then discussed her dilemma with a few friends.

"I would really like to say yes," Phoebe explained. "I have always appreciated having a devotional guide at Christmas time. I really want to help; I just would not know where to begin."

"Didn't the pastor give you any advice on how to proceed?" Sonia inquired.

"You don't know Mark very well, do you?" said Sarah. "I was in charge of Bible School last year. Mark was a great help with the kids, but our music director, Laura, was the one who really helped me get things organized."

"I know how I would start," Brenda began. "I would put a notice on the bulletin board asking people to sign up to write a devotional entry. You might get enough people to sign up without even making any phone calls, and everyone would have the same opportunity." Brenda topped it off with, "Delegation is the only way to really get things done," a comment that had become her trademark, except that this time the comment did not seem to flow naturally from her suggestion of asking for volunteers.

"I think you ought to just get a few of your friends together to write devotionals," Sarah chimed in. "I would certainly help. We don't need a reading for every day in December, two or three a week would be enough."

"I would engage the help of the Board of Christian education," Sonia suggested. "Work out a theme together for the Advent season. Consult with Mark to discover his Advent focus this year."

"If he's made up his mind yet," Sarah retorted.

Sonia went on, "Maybe even have a theme for each week of Advent. Assign a different idea and scripture to a different person for each day. It would take some work, but I think that approach would be worth your while in the long run."

A few moments ago Phoebe had a problem because she had no direction for her assignment. Now her problem was that she had too many directions. Still she liked this problem more than the previous one.

When her pastor called back in a couple of days, she told him that she would be willing to accept the assignment. Mark was delighted and made her feel good for having accepted the task. He assured her he would give her all the encouragement she needed as she progressed with the project.

A good night's sleep did not help Phoebe focus on a strategy. The next day she still pondered the three suggested options. Each seemed to have some merit. Putting a notice on the bulletin board would be simple. *But what if only two or three people signed up?* Phoebe worried. That possibility was not out of the question. People in this church would usually respond to a personal invitation, but you could never tell how well they would volunteer for tasks. During the last work day, only four had shown up to help. On the previous work day, twenty-four had come. Putting a list on the bulletin board would be a dangerous option.

Phoebe most liked the idea of working together with a few friends. This was her style, but she really didn't think that a few of them could write enough devotionals for the entire Advent season. She wasn't sure that Mark wanted a devotional book containing only a few readings.

Sonia's idea of engaging the board of Christian education was exciting. It would also be a lot of work. Phoebe did not want this one task to take away from everything else she enjoyed doing during the season. Maybe one more good night's sleep would help.

The Theory

During her lunch hour Phoebe stopped at the mall. If sleeping wouldn't help, maybe a nice window-shopping stroll would expedite her decision-making process. She paused to browse the magazine section of the bookstore.

"Excuse me," a man offered after bumping into Phoebe.

I know that voice! Phoebe thought. The gentleman's back and coat gave her no clue. She moved around to get a better angle.

"Do you have a copy of *People-Centered Leadership*, by Stephen Covey?" the man asked the clerk.

Phoebe was certain she knew that voice. He turned around.

Dr. Hastings. Yes. What a voice! Fellow students in Phoebe's undergrad organizational theory class would joke that the chairs would vibrate when Dr. Hastings got excited about a particular issue.

"Phoebe," Dr. Hastings recognized her.

"Hello," Phoebe replied.

"How are you doing, Phoebe?"

"Just fine . . . not really. I was taking a walk trying to gain some insight about . . ."

"About what?"

Dr. Hastings seemed to have some time to talk and certainly acted interested. Phoebe remembered Dr. Hastings as a professor with a welcoming smile and demeanor. She had never "picked his brain" as so many of the other students had. Organizational theory was not an area that Phoebe chose to explore in depth. She admittedly took the class upon the recommendation of a friend and because it fit her schedule that semester. She did, however, enjoy the class very much, especially Dr. Hastings's fresh and creative approach to something as dry as organizations.

"I have been asked to organize the writing and compilation of a Christmas devotional guide for our church," Phoebe explained.

"Really?"

Phoebe had forgotten how Dr. Hastings' eyebrows raised when someone mentioned the word organizing.

"Yes," she continued, "our church has previously purchased booklets from a publishing house, but the pastor thought it would be better to recruit from our own membership this year." Phoebe went on to explain Brenda's idea of posting an announcement on the bulletin board, Sarah's idea of involving a few friends, and Sonia's idea of working with the board of Christian education.

"All three ideas sound credible," Dr. Hastings replied. "Of course, each has its merits . . . and its tradeoffs."

"What do you mean?" Phoebe asked.

"Well, those three options illustrate the tradeoffs inherent among any set of solutions. No choice is perfect. Often, as is the case with your three solutions, one can see three merits: A solution is (1) general, (2) accurate, or (3) simple. A solution might have two merits, but usually not all three."[2]

"That probably explains why I am having such a hard time deciding," confessed Phoebe.

"Exactly," replied Dr. Hastings.

"General, accurate, and simple," Phoebe repeated, trying to remember.

"Yes," said Dr. Hastings. "A solution may be general and accurate; it may be general and simple; it may be simple and accurate; but rarely is a solution general, accurate, and simple all at once. In choosing the method for organizing the writing of your Christmas devotionals, you will probably have to make a tough choice."

"I know what you mean by 'simple,' but precisely what do you mean by 'general' and 'accurate'?" asked Phoebe.

"The terms will not mean the same thing in every situation," Harold began. "General could mean that the solution satisfies a great number of groups that have a vested interest in the solution; it might mean that once the solution is advertised, it will potentially appeal to a broad base of people; it might mean that the solution would be widely applicable in similar settings. In your scenario, it might mean that the solution would have ownership from a wide range of people. It seems to me that one of the goals of the church is to involve more and more people in ministry.

"The more *accurate* a solution, the closer it comes to hitting its target. In your case, the higher the quality of the finished product, the more accurate the solution. The beauty of this theory is that it reveals that 'hitting the target' is not the only consideration in choosing a solution from among the alternatives."

"That's right," Phoebe replied. "We already had an accurate solution when we used to purchase our devotional guides from a publishing house. Apparently Mark saw the need to raise the level of importance of some of the other factors to be considered in this decision.

"Even though I still have a decision to make, you have been very helpful today, Dr. Hastings," said Phoebe. "Where in the world did you get such a theory?"

"Actually, Phoebe, I covered all of that in one of my lectures, but that was a long time ago, and I wouldn't expect you to remember. It was good seeing you. One more thing, Phoebe, if we happen to run into each other again, call me Harold."

"Thank you," Phoebe replied, "for everything."

On the way back to work, Phoebe was indeed able to match her three choices to the three tradeoffs suggested by Dr. Hastings. The bulletin board approach would be the general and simple approach, yet not very accurate. Who knows what the response would be? Involving the board of Christian education would be general and accurate, but it certainly would not be simple. Teaming with a few friends to write devotionals would produce an accurate solution. It would also be relatively simple. It would not, however, be general, as it involves only a few people.

Past Application

For the past several years, the church I pastor has developed a devotional guide for use by our members. We have tried approaches similar to the three suggested by Phoebe's friends. The first year we made a broad general appeal through the newsletter, the bulletin, and pulpit announcements, inviting all to submit devotions. Six people from a 325 resident-member congregation volunteered to turn in a devotional reading. Only five were actually received. This method was general and simple. It was not, however, accurate. This approach did not obtain the type of devotional guide desired.

It is important to view solutions that do not produce desired results as learning experiences rather than failures. This first attempt of ours did have merit. Every church looks for general and simple solutions. But through analysis and evaluation, an organization can determine whether the omitted merits are too important to be sacrificed. The next time that particular event or project is tackled, the one choosing the method should consider an alternative approach, one that includes the merit originally omitted. Of course, the decision makers will have the fresh problem of deciding which other yardstick to sacrifice.

Choosing the most important merits—general, accurate, or simple—is not the same as searching for the perfect solution. Churches are more prone than other organizations to suffer from a "perfection syndrome," a condition that influences an organization to search for perfect solutions. Have you ever heard something like this: "Surely in our church, we can find an adequate solution to this problem"? But how is one defining the word adequate? My definition of adequate solution acknowledges that one must sacrifice one (the least desired) of these three merits. Another person may be looking for a solution that sacrifices nothing—the perfect solution.

These two definitions portray two differing assumptions about organizations. Church leaders often assume that perfect solutions will be available, if only we think and pray long and hard enough. While thinking and praying should be a part of any church decision, it would benefit church leaders to change their assumptions about the flawlessness of available decisions. Recognizing that decision making involves tradeoffs challenges one of our basic assumptions about organizing and decision making. It challenges the assumption that perfect decisions are available.

Challenging assumptions can make people uncomfortable. Change itself hurts. Changing assumptions involves more than an attitude shift; it involves a shift in viewpoint. Shifting our perceptions about organizations is a more difficult assignment than giving in to your solution over mine. It is more difficult because it means that the next time the group discusses any solution about the organization, members of the group will have to keep in mind the new viewpoint, namely that any solution will involve tradeoffs. It would be much easier to give in to your solution without trying to understand your reasoning behind it. The problem with this is that the next time we discuss a solution, we will probably be at opposite sides again, torn between searching for the perfect solution and accepting the limitation of tradeoffs.

Another real problem with challenging assumptions involves language. The vocabulary of the organizational assumptions held by the majority sounds very logical and rational. The problem is that there are no pleasant sounding alternatives for words like logical and rational. Now that you've read this chapter, imagine a discussion with one of your fellow church leaders.

Suppose that you are discussing a very complicated issue when you remember this chapter. "I have just read this book that suggests that there are no perfect solutions," you say. Hearing no reply, you continue,

"The book suggested that there are always tradeoffs to consider when searching for solutions."

Following a pregnant pause, another church leader responds, "So, now you expect us to look for imperfect solutions?" Language is one of the major weaknesses for nonorthodox organizational theorists who choose to debate other organizational theorists who still hold on to the dominant organizational theory paradigm. People who hold different assumptions about organizations often speak about their organizations in dramatically different ways.

In challenging someone's assumptions, it is helpful to propose new language for the new assumptions. In discussing tradeoffs among solutions it may be helpful to introduce the word complete as opposed to the word imperfect. Matthew 5:48 says, "Be perfect, therefore, as your heavenly Father is perfect." The word *teleioi*, which is translated as *perfect*, can also be rendered *complete*. It means to bring to an end or bring to its goal or accomplishment. The same root word is translated as *finished* when, upon the cross, Jesus states, "It is finished" (John 19:30). Although Jesus' life was nearly finished, Jesus may have been more appropriately implying that he had completed his tasks. The word is also used in 1 John 4:18 when we discover that "perfect" love casts out fear. It makes more sense for me to aim toward "complete" rather than "perfect" love for others. Many find it theologically trying to think that Christ demands us to be as perfect as God in heaven. We would find it less trying to be complete persons. In suggesting to a group that there may be no perfect solution, one might quickly add that the job of the group should be to find the most complete solution available.

Future Application

Church leaders may apply the General-Accurate-Simple (GAS) formulation to any situation in search of a solution. In listing all possible solutions, often a group will neglect a portion of the GAS formulation. The group may fail to consider a solution that is general and accurate but not simple, or a solution that is accurate and simple but not general. A group may apply this theory in searching for every possible resolution.

One of our solar system's nine recognized planets was discovered by someone who knew where to look. A scientist had devised a formula for the distances between the planets. The formula proved correct except for a "gap" between two of the planets. If his theory was correct, there was a planet that had not yet been discovered. The planet Neptune was discovered by knowing precisely where to aim the telescope. Perfect solutions may not exist. The most complete solutions possible for a specific situation, however, may be discovered by knowing where to look amid the gaps.

Using This Chapter with a Small Group

1. Ask the group to suggest a problem suitable for applying the GAS formulation. Consider a situation that many people are interested in and that has a great number of possible solutions.

2. Decide which two of the three merits—general, accurate, and simple—are the most important.

3. Use traditional brainstorming techniques for suggesting possible solutions, being careful not to criticize anyone's suggestion.

4. Categorize each possible solution into one of three areas: general and accurate, accurate and simple, or simple and general.

5. Choose the most appropriate solution from among those that satisfy the criteria chosen in step 2.

6. If time allows, repeat the process using a different problem.

7. As an alternative, the group may analyze previous solutions to an old problem in light of the GAS formulation. Did the solution chosen minimize the least desired merit? Does the GAS theory suggest any new solutions—filling in any previously neglected "gaps" along the GAS continuum?

CHAPTER II

The Loop Theory: Learning to Break or Enhance a Cycle

The Scenario

Phoebe sat in her Sunday school class determined to grasp the morning's lesson. Dr. Shaw, the teacher, was extremely knowledgeable—about the Bible, about world issues, current events, community happenings, even court cases. He presented new ideas for consideration. The problem for Phoebe was that the erudite Dr. Shaw was, well, less than exciting as a teacher. Phoebe knew she was not alone in her feelings. Upon leaving class, one of her friends would often whisper, "I sure didn't get a glove on that one today, did you?"

Dr. Shaw never used any curriculum. He would twine together columns and editorials from the newspaper, *US News and World Report*, and the Bible. Today's lesson focused on environmental issues. Phoebe had much personal interest in the topic. Yet she became more disinterested with each passing minute. And every week the pattern was the same. She began the session with good intentions, but methodically and almost hypnotically her mind drifted away; her ability to make an intelligent comment decreased as did her understanding of the material when she "came back" to the group. Her lack of understanding increased her level of boredom making her feel even further away from the lesson. An endless cycle transpired on a weekly basis.

Each adult Sunday school class at First Church chose its own teacher. Every year Dr. Shaw was the only one to volunteer to teach Phoebe's class. "No one would dare upend the endowed teaching chair of Dr. Shaw," Phoebe's friend remarked. There seemed to be an assumption that the ones with the most knowledge should shoulder the role of teacher, regardless of actual teaching expertise. Phoebe had a feeling there should be exceptions to that rule, especially for her class, but was afraid to express her concerns to anyone. Lesson after lesson, Dr. Shaw taught Phoebe's class. Lesson after lesson, Phoebe spiraled down the cycle of boredom.

Options

Each week Phoebe would leave her Sunday school class frustrated in her attempts to get something from the lesson. Usually her anxieties would ease after a few days. This week was different. The uneasiness didn't go away. Each time something reminded her of church, her mind would race toward the dilemma of the Sunday school class. She thought about the issue over two days. As she drove to her cell group meeting, she contemplated various options. Every option seemed to have too many drawbacks.

Several members of her cell group were also members of her class. Maybe these friends could help, if Phoebe could find the right way to raise the issue.

Late in the evening, during refreshments, Phoebe realized she hadn't brought up the topic of Sunday school, though she still intended to.

Then Sonia asked her a question, in the presence of Sarah and Brenda. "Phoebe, I hear you involved the board of Christian education in your devotional guide preparation. Wasn't that my idea when Sarah, Brenda, you, and I discussed it?"

"It did turn out nice," Brenda admitted.

"Yes, I thought it was lovely and very thought provoking," Sarah matched. "Someone remarked that the pastor used some of the writings for his radio devotions the week before Christmas. That's good for our church."

"We were pleased with the results," said Phoebe, "but it was a lot of hard work. It took time away from other activities that I am usually involved in at Christmas time. Still, I guess it was worth it—seeing the final product in hand."

Sonia offered, "I think a lot of people found the piece inspiring."

"Speaking of inspiring," Brenda remarked with a hint of sarcasm, "what did you think of Dr. Shaw's Sunday school lecture?"

How in the world did that happen? wondered Phoebe. She didn't even have to raise the issue herself.

"I'm sure he knew what he was talking about," Sarah replied, "but I don't think many others did. Dull. Dry. Someone just needs to talk to him. It's not fair to us to sit through those types of lessons. This year, when it comes time to reelect our teacher, I plan to say something. I'm not saying I would teach, but I think someone else besides Dr. Shaw needs to try."

"We don't want to hurt his feelings," remarked Sonia. "Maybe we could try a team teaching situation. Some of the other Sunday school classes do that."

Phoebe added, "Actually I have been thinking about this for two days. I wonder if there would be a way to hint to Dr. Shaw that he needs to attend a teacher training event. Even if we went to a team teaching approach, I'm afraid I would dread the class every time Dr. Shaw's turn came around."

"I don't think he would go for training," returned Sarah. "Besides, I think we need a total change, a clean break."

"Maybe each of us could do more to prepare ourselves for the class," Phoebe said, as she offered another option she had been weighing. "Sometimes, like last Sunday, I am very interested in Dr. Shaw's topic. But even when I desperately want to listen, I start down a cycle of boredom. Maybe there are some things I could do to break that cycle."

"We could drink ten cups of coffee for breakfast," Sarah said. "That might keep us awake."

"We could ask Larry to set his watch to beep every five minutes instead of just on the hour," added Brenda.

"Something needs to be done," they all agreed.

The Theory

After the cell group meeting, something made Phoebe recall her recent conversation with Dr. Hastings—Harold. She walked over to the bookcase, and, yes, found a copy of her organizational theory textbook. She was surprised she had not sold it for a few dollars to someone taking the course the next semester. As she perused the pages, she was glad she had not sold it. Although she'd previously highlighted very few pages, she now underlined scattered phrases. She even found the GAS theory, which Dr. Hastings had outlined in the bookstore.

While leafing through the pages, Phoebe discovered something that applied to her new dilemma—searching for options to improve her Sunday school class. She stumbled onto a section, "Causal Loops and Control." She read and garnered a simple understanding of a causal loop, describing the scenario when someone says, "Every time I get involved in that situation, the same thing happens. . . . "

"You will find," she read, "that the variable you started with increases even further once you have completed the circuit and it continues to increase every time you complete the cycle . . . until the system is destroyed or until some dramatic change occurs."[1]

Phoebe could remember Dr. Hastings saying in his lecture, "A variable is something that can be changed." She remembered his animated presentation about people who are often unwilling to try to change a situation that can indeed be altered with proper intervention. Phoebe needed to change some of the variables in her situation.

This loop theory matched Phoebe's situation perfectly. Entering the Sunday school class was entering a loop with five variables. Not long after sitting down, her level of *boredom* increased. The boredom decreased her *understanding*. Her lack of understanding lowered her positive feelings for Dr. Shaw. The lowering of these *feelings* decreased her *willingness to comment*. Reducing her willingness to comment minimized her *sense of connection* with the rest of the students and her level of boredom heightened a little from where it had been a few minutes before, at the beginning of the cycle. The cycle repeated, her level of boredom increasing a little each time she completed a circuit.

While this loop theory did not actually provide Phoebe with a solution to her problem, it did instill the notion that something would have to be done to break the cycle. This benefit alone can be priceless. Many times the sole reason for inaction in organizations is assuming that a situation will take care of itself. Idleness is chosen over breaking the loop, often because breaking the loop has at least one possible negative effect. Church leaders seldom jeopardize the short-term atmosphere for long-term gain. Following traditional organizational patterns prevents church leaders from being risk takers.

Sometimes church leaders would do better to break traditional patterns and take a chance. Even tentative action is preferable to inaction when a negative situation appears to be cyclical. The cyclical na-ture of the scenario ensures that the dilemma will get worse and worse instead of better and better. Left to solve itself, a solution will usually come in the form of disintegration or explosion of the entire loop. In the case of Phoebe's Sunday school class, if nothing is done to improve the situation, the class will likely dissolve as one by one the members move to another class, stop coming to Sunday school, or join another church. Or, if nothing is done, someone in the class could easily blow his or her top in the middle of one of the lessons. In most instances, an action that causes a few adverse consequences is preferable to disintegration or an explosion. Indeed, churches and Sunday school classes have been known to explode or disintegrate.

How was Phoebe to break the loop that produced negative feelings? Her friends in the cell group had offered a variety of suggestions. Many were humorous; a few were plausible.

She planned a strategy that began with herself. Every time she felt her boredom increase, she was going to try to break the loop. She could shift her weight, take notes, look up a related passage of scripture, or, if necessary, excuse herself to the restroom.

Second, she would talk to Dr. Shaw, for herself but on behalf of the others in the class who would likely not implement personal strategies to stay interested. She decided sincerity coupled with tact was the best approach for Dr. Shaw, a person who seemed to like things straight on. She would begin by revealing her great interest in many of the topics but then state that sometimes she could not grasp what he was saying about the day's topic. She knew this strategy could have some negative results, but at least it was a strategy to break the loop.

Phoebe had devised a two-stage strategy. Her first step sought to add another variable—physical activity—to the loop. Shifting her weight and taking notes are examples of physical activity. Her second step attempted to change the "boredom" variable by altering the source of the boredom, namely, Dr. Shaw's presentation style. Adding variables and adjusting variables are both means of influencing the cycle.

As with each chapter in this book, this theory challenges a widely held assumption about organizations. While the GAS theory, discussed in the previous chapter, challenged the assumption that there can be perfect solutions to problems within the organization, the loop theory challenges the assumption that organizations are linear. The life of a congregation is sometimes more like sitting on a merry-go-round or driving in a road race than pressing on toward higher ground.

The loop theory also challenges the assumption that risk takers do not belong in church leadership. Church leaders sometimes need to make a bold statement and then maintain a steadfast presence in facing the consequences. When church leaders can discover only options that are potentially hazardous in the short run, they prefer to do nothing and maintain the status quo. But there is no status quo in the church. The church is a living organism that is either growing or deteriorating. Church leaders have a responsibility to allow the Spirit of God to breathe new life and growth into the congregation. Sometimes this means pruning a negative cyclical situation.

Past Application

Similar to Phoebe, I have applied the loop theory several times when faced with boredom as a student. I have taken more aggressive notes, revised my to-do list for the next day, or sought out the nearest available coffee pot. The classroom situation is one of the most common places to discover loops.

Not long into my pastorate I discovered a different kind of loop occurring in one of our Bible study discussion classes. The loop commenced with someone raising a question. Another member of the group would comment upon the raised question. Still others would add to the discussion. The discussion would continue to progress. If polarized comments surfaced, however, someone would quickly ask, "Pastor, what do you think?" An observer could have predicted within seconds how long it would take someone to solicit the pastor's opinion once two differing comments had surfaced. If I declined to comment, the discussion would go one more round, increasing the urgency of the group's request for the pastor's insight.

I sensed within the group a strong need to understand the "right answer" to the question. Yet I believe that there is often no one right answer to Bible questions. A part of the beauty of scripture is its deliberately ambiguous nature, allowing two persons in two very different situations to glean something helpful from the same passage.

To break this loop, one week I established three ground rules for

the group: (1) We would pray for the Holy Spirit to guide each individual's understanding of the text. (2) Our first priority in the group
would be to listen and seek to understand what others were saying. (3)
We would never seek to change someone else's opinion. These ground
rules broke the loop that had previously ended with a summons for the
pastor.

Future Application

Loops can occur virtually anywhere within an organization. Loops may
occur between two people, among family members, in any group or
committee situation, and within churches. One of the most dangerous
negative loops is through the "grapevine" news network within the
church. The "telephone tag" distortion can further the harmful effects of
a grapevine loop.

Another dangerous and common negative loop surfaces among
church staff. In nearly every church situation, there will be parishioners
whom the pastor has not "connected with" in a strong way. The occa-
sion of a new staff person can be an opportunity for additional people to
be pastored within a congregation. It is also, however, an opportunity
for conflict to result from a causal loop.

As church members get to know the new staff person, at some
point one will say something about appreciating the staff person more
than the senior pastor. Another person may reveal a weakness about the
pastor while confiding in the staff person. The staff person may not
even agree with the comment. But if she or he listens to the comment,
news of this has a way of finding its way to the senior pastor. Resent-
ment between the pastor and staff person slowly surfaces. The resent-
ment makes it more likely for the staff person to listen to more negative
comments about the pastor. The loop continues over and over until the
relationship between the pastor and staff person disintegrates into iso-
lation or explosion. One way to stop this loop from ever beginning is
to create a covenant among all of the pastors and staff that no one will
listen to negative comments about any of the others. Rather, parishioners are encouraged to channel concerns through a personnel committee.

Loops may not always present negative results. In contrast to the
loop experienced by Phoebe, a "positive" loop might exist in a Sunday

school class. The loop might cycle each time to raise the level of interest of the students. Loops with positive results often occur in worship services, small groups, and other arenas.

A loop may even turn into an entire movement. Gerlach and Hine define a religious movement employing language that could be analyzed using the causal loop theory. They describe such a movement as

> a group of people who are organized for, ideologically motivated by, and committed to a purpose which implements some form of personal or social change; who are actively engaged in the recruitment of others; and whose influence is spreading in opposition to the established order within which it originated.[2]

The elements of this loop or movement might be recruitment, assimilation, discipling, and recruitment again by the newest disciples.

In the same way the loops with negative results can be broken, loops with positive results can be created or enhanced. In seeking to devise a new loop to produce positive results, one should analyze the loop regularly to ensure that each element is contributing to the cycle. Once a loop with positive results is successfully implemented, the desired results will escalate. Studying the phenomena of loops gives the church leader a concrete way to enhance a positive situation or effectively intervene in a negative one.

Using This Chapter with a Small Group

1.   Ask the group to think of a situation that may contain a causal loop. Has anyone ever said, "Every time I attend this committee meeting, run into this person, or get involved in this situation, I get this same feeling or result"?

2.   Choose one situation and list the effects that surface each time the person encounters that situation.

3.   Make connections among the variables. To do this, ask: Do any of these variables affect any of the other variables? What influence does increasing or decreasing a new variable have on another variable? Portray the connections between the variables with arrows. Continue forming a loop until you can no longer include any of the remaining "uninfluenced variables" into the loop.

4.   You will probably discover gaps, places where there is no connection with one of the variables. When you get to a place where you cannot make a connection, ask: Besides what we've already listed, what else occurs when this variable is influenced? New variables will probably surface; add them to the loop. Try to link them to unconnected variables. One asset of this theory is that it allows the group to discover hidden variables. Do not set aside unconnected variables until you have searched for new, hidden variables.

5.   After identifying a loop, brainstorm possible ideas to influence it. If the group has chosen a loop with positive results, discuss ways to enhance it. If the group has chosen a loop with negative results, discuss ways of breaking the loop. Try adding new variables and influence existing variables.

6.   Test the merit of each idea by considering its consequences on each variable in the cycle. Which idea most enhances the positive loop or most limits the negative loop?

CHAPTER III

The Pareto Principle: Leading a Few to Lead Others

The Scenario

Laura Fisher passed Phoebe, who was humming as she slowly walked down a church hallway. "You're certainly in a good mood today, Phoebe," Laura posed. For three years Laura had served as minister of Christian education and music at First Church. In her early forties, Laura was a tamed maverick. In her college days, she had been "sounder of the trumpet" for the rallying cries of the world. As the rest of the baby boomers caught up with her causes, she learned to discipline her drive and work cooperatively in making a difference. For Laura, the mission of the church began at the front door. Others were beginning to share her convictions, having experienced the coldness of the world outside of the church. She had learned to be zealous toward her cause but cautious in her approach. Laura had learned the realities of the church, which posts its "slow moving vehicle" sign every time someone mentions the word *change*.

"You must have had a good Sunday school class today," Laura said to Phoebe, who continued to hum as they continued down the hall.

"Yes," Phoebe responded. "I had been having trouble understanding Dr. Shaw's lessons. But after reviewing an old textbook and identifying problems and solutions, I marshaled the courage to talk to him."

"How did it go?" Laura questioned with curiosity.

"Okay, I guess," said Phoebe. "He didn't say much as I talked to him. He's often hard to read anyway. My instincts tell me that it will work out in the long run. I had no trouble paying attention today. I'd gotten into a downward cycle every time I entered the classroom.

Today, when I started to lose interest, I tried to break the cycle of boredom. Right after that, Dr. Shaw actually divided the class into small discussion groups. He had never done that before. I really think the interest in the class will pick up."

"Where did you find the textbook resource?" Laura asked.

"It was an organizational theory textbook used by Dr. Hastings, a former professor of mine," Phoebe explained. "I ran into him in the mall one day. He explained how to approach the Christmas devotional booklets. And then the textbook gave me some answers to my Sunday school class problem."

"I sure wish I could find a new strategy to get more excitement into the Sunday school class I teach," Laura said.

"The high school students?"

"Yes," Laura responded. "Some of them don't participate much. I've tried lots of creative approaches, but nothing seems to work. Sometimes I spend so much time drawing out the nonparticipants, I'm afraid I bore the ones who are interested."

"If you're already trying creative teaching techniques, I don't think you simply need to break a negative cycle of boredom, as I saw the problem in my class," Phoebe said, trying to console Laura. "You must be experiencing a different kind of problem."

"I wonder if your professor friend might have some insights to offer for my situation." Laura's mind had been circling the possibilities ever since Phoebe had mentioned her professor friend. She was ready to stop the wagons and shoot the question. "Would you care if I called Dr. Hastings?"

"I don't know if he would mind or not," Phoebe answered. "Why don't you let me approach him first?"

"Sure," said Laura. "If he is interested in consulting, I'm sure we could offer him something for his time."

Options

Each week Laura approached her class determined to draw in those who came but showed little interest. Many people had remarked about Laura's imaginative teaching style. She would present lessons in "game show" format, adapting the presentation of the material to "Hollywood

Squares" and "Family Feud." Once a stranger covered with a blanket came to the classroom to help Laura teach the story of the healing of the ten lepers. She had incorporated small groups and skits, taken field trips, and served refreshments. Still, some of the students displayed very little interest in the weekly lessons. Laura was frustrated because she could not equally engage every student.

School teachers hold differing opinions about the concept of mastery learning—the view that there are certain principles and abilities that every student should possess upon graduating from school.[1] Mastery learning poses this dilemma: How much is a teacher willing to sacrifice the interest of those who grasp the concept quickly in order to make sure that every student in the room understands? Some argue that our adult literacy problem is due in part to a lack of emphasis upon mastery learning.[2] Others argue that too much emphasis upon mastery learning has resulted in lower achievement scores, especially at the top end of the scale.[3]

The mastery learning dilemma within public schools can also be applied to Christian education. A typical Sunday school class includes students with a wide range of interests and abilities. As in public schools, denominations see certain principles as important for members to comprehend. The church also has the responsibility of providing opportunities for every member to mature. Shouldn't every member of a church be stronger in faith and have more knowledge of God this year than the previous year?

A widely held assumption is that organizations, especially churches, must involve everyone. The church should be the one place where everyone is accepted and allowed to progress at her or his own pace. Pastors are asked to prepare sermons that appeal to the masses. Teachers are required to teach to the whole spectrum of interest and ability. The most popular guest speakers do more to inspire than to build frameworks for future growth and intellectual development. When the leadership constantly appeals to the populace, a church often stagnates, resembling the one that stood on that street corner twenty-five years before.

Must a church involve everyone to the same degree? One theory, the Pareto principle, suggests otherwise. This theory calls for churches or groups within a church to focus on the segment showing the most interest. Sometimes a church grows best by feeding the green stuff, rather than by constantly trying to make the brown stuff come alive.

The Theory

That week Phoebe called Dr. Hastings. She thanked him for his help on
the Christmas devotional booklets. "I ended up pursuing the general and
accurate approach. It was a lot of hard work, but the finished product
made it all worthwhile. After Christmas, I tackled another problem with
the aid of another organizational theory. I decided to do something about
my Sunday school class. Armed with information about cycles of boredom, I approached my teacher and had a very productive conversation."

"That's great, Phoebe," replied Harold. "I didn't realize you had
taken such a sudden interest in organizational theory."

"I guess I didn't always see the practical applications when you
covered them in class," Phoebe confessed. "Now, I am really getting interested in this field. I was explaining some of the material to Laura, our
minister of Christian education and music. She needs help with her Sunday school class and asked if I thought you would give her some ideas."

"What's her predicament?" Harold asked.

"It's the high school class. Several students come regularly but
show little interest despite her varied teaching approach. She goes to
great lengths to draw these kids in, so much so that she's afraid she is
not paying enough attention to those who are interested." Phoebe
paused to detect the tone in Harold's voice. *Was he bothered, being
asked for advice?*

"It's the eighty-twenty principle," Harold responded enthusiasti-
cally. Phoebe hadn't caught on that Harold would rather talk about the
applications of organizational theory than anything else. Harold was a
practical theorist. He liked to read and develop new theories, but, more,
he liked to apply them to real-world situations. He could apply the findings of organizational theorists to a wide variety of settings, including
the church.

"The eighty-twenty principle?" Phoebe questioned.

"Yes," Harold continued. "It is also called the Pareto principle.
Laura has probably been able to involve about 20 percent of her class in
a significant way. She would undoubtedly like to involve the other 80
percent. For years, leaders have tried to involve 'the other 80 percent.'
The eighty-twenty—Pareto—principle simply breaks down a group of
people into a four-to-one ratio and then seeks to make some distinction
about the two subgroups.

"You can see applications of the Pareto principle every day. Twenty percent of the items in a grocery store will usually produce 80 percent of the profits. I read an article the other day where an accountant had applied the Pareto principle to his clients. He started with the assumption that the top 20 percent of his clients produced 80 percent of his profits. He then further divided the top 20 percent of his clients into two subgroups who respectively produced 50 percent and 30 percent of his profits. He then analyzed three classes of clients: class A, which produced 50 percent of the results; class B, which produced 30 percent of the results; and class C, which produced 20 percent of the results in his business."[4]

Phoebe did not interrupt.

"The Pareto principle," Harold explained, "has been around a long time. Another application is that 80 percent of the population usually considers themselves to be in the top 20 percent of whatever category you may choose to discuss. To put it another way, 80 percent of the teachers in the world consider themselves to be in the top 20 percent of all teachers. That is what makes it so difficult to conduct merit reviews in school settings and other organizations."

"That is what made it so hard to talk to Dr. Shaw about his teaching," Phoebe commented aloud.

"What was that?" inquired Harold.

"Oh, nothing," Phoebe said, "please go on."

"As I was saying, the Pareto principle has circulated for centuries," Harold explained. "It has only recently been revived in relation to leadership issues. You can tell Laura that I would be glad to have her call me to discuss this principle in greater detail."

Phoebe relayed Harold's insights to Laura. It did not take Laura long to call him.

"Dr. Hastings?"

"Yes."

"This is Laura Fisher. Phoebe Romans suggested I might phone you and ask you a few questions about my Sunday school class."

"Yes, I told her you could call. Tell me a little about your class. High schoolers?"

"Yes, when I started with the class about three months ago, a few of the students jumped right in and were 'with' me. But I haven't been able to get any of the others interested."

"What have you tried?" asked Harold.

Laura detailed the list of gimmicks and games she had used to make the class interesting to every student.

"About how many students are in the class?"

"We average twelve. Only three or four are really involved."

"Have you tried working with the three or four who show the most interest—using them to get the remaining students more interested?" asked Harold.

"What do you mean?" Laura quizzed.

"There is an ancient theory that suggests that only 20 percent of a group will fully invest in the group," Harold explained. "And one of the new leadership ideas is to train the dedicated 20 percent to help involve the other 80 percent. You might try capitalizing on the interest of the three or four; as they grow, they can help you absorb the other eight or nine into the class flow. Teachers in other settings have tried student or peer teaching, student discipling, or working one-on-one with the few most interested to allow them to grow, and placing the ones most interested as leaders of subgroups.

"Another thing you might do is not try so hard," Harold advised.

"Not try so hard?" asked Laura.

"If you can lower your expectation that each of the students should be involved equally, you can release some of your anxiety," Harold explained. "As new students graduate from the class and others come in, the atmosphere will change. The eighty-twenty principle is a phenomenon that your particular class seems to be experiencing in a strong way, but the theory does not hold true for every classroom situation. A lot depends on the mix of students. Things may be very different for you next year."

"This is the first time I've experienced such a high level of disinterest. But are you suggesting that there will always be some students who choose not to participate as strongly as others?"

"Yes, that is a part of what I am saying," said Harold.

"I guess the level of the apathy is what has alarmed me this time," Laura concluded.

"The eighty-twenty principle is a clandestine part of life," Harold said philosophically. "Realizing and accepting the theory can avoid a lot of headaches."

"It certainly will," Laura said. Once again, Laura's drive to be perfect in her endeavors had been tamed. She would begin to accept some realistic limits for her classroom. She had received encouragement to redirect her efforts in a way that could produce positive results. She would accept the fact that every student was not going to be as interested as Myron, who seemed so hungry to learn. She would use Myron and the others who were interested to bring out the potential—even if limited —in the rest of the class.

Past Application

While the New Testament church involved everyone in the community life, training a few to train others is also a biblical commission. Jesus spent much of his three-year ministry with a small group of twelve disciples. One may also point to small groups of deacons, priests, apostles, elders, and bishops trained to lead others.

Church growth proponents have claimed success for the eighty-twenty principle in recent years. "Spend 80 percent of your time with the top 20 percent of your membership," they tell pastors. Others have lifted up the imagery of church leadership being more like a rancher than a shepherd. A shepherd does the leading himself, while a rancher trains others to lead. In addition to focusing on people, some also apply the principle to tasks. In his *Ten Steps to Breaking the 200 Barrier*, Bill Sullivan includes a chapter titled, "Focus on the Critical Few."[5] He advocates centering on a few activities aimed at church growth rather than trying several activities simultaneously. Church growth advocates are calling for pastors to focus on 20 percent of their congregation to lead the other 80 percent. They claim that this is a strategy that will lead to church growth.

While this aspect of the eighty-twenty principle is intriguing to many, it does not appear without warnings on its label. Working extensively with a small group of church members can lead to a "church within the church" or what Philipp Spener terms an "ecclesiola in ecclesia."[6] Howard Snyder articulates this warning, "Whether such ecclesiolae can in fact function without creating factions or schisms, and whether it is ever legitimate to allow for what may amount to two levels of discipleship in the church, are two major questions raised by the ecclesiola approach."[7]

As the church leadership begins to train those willing to train others, the leadership must maintain an open door between the laity who train and the laity who are trained; that is, anyone willing to commit the time necessary to learn how to train others in the church should be given that opportunity.

In summary, there are two keys to this theory: (1) not expecting the same from everyone and (2) training those who are willing to invest the most time and resources to lead others. But leadership must guard against ignoring the talents of any. By enlisting the help of those most willing to serve, leaders must seek out ways for all to use their spiritual gifts.

Future Application

The eighty-twenty principle has a wide variety of applications. Many groups or organizations may be meaningfully subdivided into two groups with a four-to-one ratio between the groups. In many congregations 20 percent of the membership will give 80 percent of the budget. Some pastors claim that 20 percent of their church's membership accomplishes 80 percent of the work. Twenty percent of a pastor's goals will often accomplish 80 percent of the changes she or he hopes to attain from the entire set of goals. Some pastors would do well to focus 80 percent of their efforts on 20 percent of the tasks that are most meaningful and result producing. In yet another application, Kennon Callahan uses a seventy-thirty formula to make a point about missional versus institutional organizations. In his advocacy for mission-minded churches, he says that a missional organization will focus 70 percent of its leadership on the outside world and 30 percent inside the organization, while an institutional organization will reverse the ratios.[8]

Using This Chapter with a Small Group

1.   Begin with an exercise. Ask group members to rate themselves personally in a particular category. Examples might include leadership ability, Christian maturity, physical reflexes, decision-making expertise, and so forth. Group members should rate themselves in a percentile grouping: 0 to 20, 20 to 40, 40 to 60, 60 to 80, or 80 to 100 percent compared to all other people. Compile the results. What percentage of the group rated themselves in the top 20 percent? How close does this result match the eighty-twenty principle? (For greatest impact, this exercise might be done prior to the assignment of reading chapter 3.)

2.   The leader might also want to compile other church figures in advance of the meeting to demonstrate the reality of the eighty-twenty principle, including church finances and percentage of membership that holds church offices and board positions.

3.   Discuss the reality, impact, limitations, and surprises of the eighty-twenty principle.

4.   Discuss creative leadership training ideas for those already involved in various groups, Sunday school classes, and ministries.

5.   Discuss specific ideas for how Laura might use the three or four interested students to get the rest of the class more interested.

CHAPTER IV

The Myers-Briggs Type Indicator: Discovering the Gifts of All

The Scenario

Every church has an unofficial gathering place where people mill around and share bits of information that do not fit in a Bible study, cell group, iphone conversation, or sermon. For many churches the place is right inside the front door. Others have a room with an official title, such as parlor, narthex, or foyer.

The concept is as old as the patriarchs. In the book of Genesis, Abraham's servant seemed to know where to go to look for a bride for Isaac. Later, in searching for his own bride, Jacob had no trouble finding a gathering place. After being out of town a few days, every pastor knows which coffee shop to visit first to catch up on the news.

Phoebe, Laura, Jack (the Sunday school teacher for college age students), and a few other people had assembled in an area just outside the kitchen, the "gathering place" for people at First Church.

Phoebe and Laura discussed their recent conquests in the Sunday school arena. Phoebe's teacher, Dr. Shaw, had continued to introduce new techniques into his lesson plans and the class had responded positively. Laura had subdivided her class into noncompetitive teams and carefully chosen the leaders for each team. Each had certain responsibilities based on the gifts of the team. Laura had used some ideas from a business class she had taken on Total Quality Management (TQM). The ideas had proved beneficial in making the class more interesting and getting more of the students involved.

Jack had been listening to their conversation. "I sure wish I could witness a renewal in my class," he declared. "I have listened to the types of problems you encountered and the solutions you came up with and it sounds great. But the problems I am experiencing are different from either of yours."

"Like what?" questioned Laura.

"There doesn't seem to be a lack of interest or involvement in my class," Jack continued. "The students are attentive and raise good questions. Nearly every Sunday the students leave the class in a good mood, often discussing the topic as they walk out of the room. The problem is . . . well, the students and I just seem to have different aims for what we should be accomplishing in the class. They leave happy about what occurred. I leave frustrated. "

"Why?" queried Phoebe.

"For instance, I think it is important to integrate the lesson ideas into each person's own philosophy," Jack said. "I regularly talk about how to apply the material or principle to their lives. To me, application is one of the most salient portions of the entire lesson, but it doesn't seem to be of much interest to my students. Also, I try to begin with an overview of the lesson. I don't see how they can grasp any of the details until I give them the overall direction of where we are headed that day. But none of them pays attention to the overview. I get the feeling they would rather I just started in with section one, but that would be hard for me."

Phoebe, Laura, and others listened to Jack's predicament, but no one seemed to have any suggestions at this point.

Jack continued, "Another thing I strive for is personal harmony. I want our class to maintain a sense of unity about the ideas presented. I tense up when there is disagreement and try my best to create compatibility in the room. But it's hard because this group seldom agrees on anything. And the disagreements don't seem to bother the rest of the class. I think that some of them actually enjoy the debating.

"And another thing," Jack said a little louder, venting his frustration, with so many eager ears listening. "I think closure is important in a class. The authors obviously have written all of the material for a reason. I get anxious when I can't cover all of the lesson material, especially the closing section. But my students? They don't seem to care how much of the lesson is covered as long as they have a chance to interact." Jack had never identified the problem so clearly before. Talking about a situation always seemed to help him clarify his thoughts.

Options

For months Jack had pondered many different reasons behind his dilemma of experiencing different goals for his class than his students. Was there a generation gap? After all, he was twenty or twenty-five years older than the students he taught. No one, however, had ever accused Jack of not relating to younger—or older—people. In fact, he thought his ability to relate was one factor in his being asked to teach this particular class. Jack did not want to accept this as the reason for the problem.

Jack could not understand how a group of students could be so different from himself. *Why can't the students value the same criteria by which I judge a good lesson?* he thought. *How can the students be so different from me and still have the capacity to enjoy the class?* He was perplexed.

Jack truly wanted his class to be more homogeneous. Some church growth proponents encourage homogeneous cell groups and even homogeneous churches. While these proponents claim success for this principle, it can be misconstrued if carried to an extreme. A great amount of diversity exists in our world today. A great amount of diversity may even exist within one group where the members appear to be similar in background. For example, many hold a false assumption that people of one ethnic background think alike.

The homogeneity concept may imply that teaching a group of people is easier than it actually is. Even when the members of a small group have similar backgrounds, other factors such as birth order, interest, vocation, family functioning and dysfunctioning, and personality cause each person to be different.

As the world continues to change, homogeneity will be a characteristic of fewer and fewer groups, churches, and Sunday school classes. The church will need to find ways to discover the diverse nature of its membership. Discovering its unique giftedness can lead to enhanced ministry and growth for everyone involved. One technique available that focuses on varied personal gifts is the Myers-Briggs personality Inventory (MBTI).

The Theory

In the church hallway everyone tried to console Jack, though no one had any concrete suggestions that day.

Later Jack's frustrations resurfaced in Laura's mind. Actually, she was able to remember nearly every word of their Sunday conversation. First of all, it was Laura's job as minister of Christian education to think about this situation. Second, she knew how delighted she felt to experience renewal in her own classroom; she wanted the same for Jack.

The more she reflected on the issue, the more ideas she had. Her thoughts eventually traveled back to a seminary class where a consultant was invited in to explain the results of a personality test called the Myers-Briggs Type Indicator. She remembered the consultant saying, "There are no right answers to this test." Those words had stuck with Laura. She had taken other personality tests that claimed to have no right answer, but when reading the results, the interpreter had pointed to an optimum level for each personality characteristic. To Laura, "optimum level" meant "right answer." She remembered the MBTI differently.

Although she had to confess that she had not really personally applied the findings of the MBTI, the principles behind it had remained with her. Maybe now was the time to resurrect some interest in the MBTI; it might help Jack to focus on some issues that contribute to the diversity among people.

A few phone calls later, Laura had orchestrated a continuing education event for the Sunday school teachers. The teachers would answer a set of survey questions to discover their own personality type. A consultant would then come and interpret the results. Laura's thinking was that if each teacher became more aware of his or her own unique personality, he or she might be more appreciative of others who were different. She especially hoped Jack would attend.

The continuing education evening event was led by Phil, a priest in the community who made regular use of the MBTI. He used the survey in a number of ways including premarital counseling and small groups and in assigning committees and task forces.

Phil passed out a result sheet to each individual, revealing each one's personality type. The results of the survey revealed one's placement along four continua:

Extrovert...........................Introvert
Sensing.............................Intuitive
Thinking...........................Feeling
Judging............................Perceiving

Jack was an ENFJ—extrovert, intuitive, feeling, judging. Phoebe was an ENTJ—extrovert, intuitive, thinking, judging. Mark was an ESFP—extrovert, sensing, feeling, perceiving. Laura was an INTJ—introvert, intuitive, thinking, judging. Nearly everyone present represented a different type within the sixteen possibilities. After the participants had a chance to read a brief explanation of each category and a description of their specific personality type, Phil introduced the first category. "Imagine you have just returned home from a party. To unwind, would you sit down and read the newspaper or discuss the party with your spouse or friend?"

The group was split in their responses. Phil went on to explain that extroverts often need to unwind by acting on their environments. Introverts, however, unwind by spending time alone, or taking in information from their environments. Extroverts possess the gift of the breadth of things, and this gift draws them out into the world. Introverts, conversely, possess the gift of the depth of things. "Whichever side of the spectrum you fall on," Phil continued, "it is like being right-handed or left-handed. You will use the gifts and characteristics associated with both extroversion and introversion, but you will prefer one over the other, especially in new or stressful situations."

To introduce the next continuum, Phil placed an apple on the table. He asked participants to describe the apple. The first thing Phoebe thought of was how William Tell had placed an apple on his son's head. Her next thought was of Snow White. That was one of her favorite stories as a child. As other thoughts raced through her head, Mark, the pastor, spoke up. "It's a dark shade of red," Mark began, "and hasn't been shined up. Its stem is short. It has a nick near the bottom. I guess that is about it."

"It looks like it might be juicy and good for applesauce," Sarah chimed in. "My mother used to make applesauce every year."

"So did mine," Jack offered. "We had two apple trees on our property."

Phil used the apple to demonstrate how sensing types like Mark use their senses to describe things and take in information. Intuitives, like Jack, Phoebe, and Sarah, make connections. They continually integrate new information with other pieces. "Intuitives also have a strong need to see the 'big picture' while sensing people prefer the 'step by step' approach," Phil said.

With Phil's last statement, Jack had an "aha." Maybe his students did not seem interested in his lesson overviews because they did not need to see the big picture. While Jack was clearly an intuitive, the majority of his students might be sensing types. After all, Phil had revealed that only 25 percent of those who take the Myers-Briggs have been shown to be intuitive types. Jack's interest in this presentation suddenly increased.

To introduce the third category, Phil asked, "If this group were put in charge of the decision making for buying new chairs for your church, what should the most prominent considerations be?"

"We want them to last," Laura uttered. "We should seek out the best and most durable quality for our money."

"I agree," offered Phoebe. "We should decide on a few parameters like material and size, secure several bids, and take the lowest."

"Aren't we going to sit in these chairs?" asked Sarah. "I think that comfort and style should be a consideration in the matter. They should also match our existing decor."

"Your group has beautifully illustrated two important factors in decision making," illuminated Phil. "Thinking types make decisions according to rationality and logic."

"Then I suppose feeling types must be irrational and illogical," snickered Brenda, whose results showed her to be a strong thinking type.

"Not at all," Phil said. "One may suggest a long list of stereotypes for each type, but we are here to focus on the gifts associated with each. Feeling types make decisions based on what people value, what they consider to be important. You can see what type of chair a committee comprised totally of thinking types might purchase. It might last forever but not be very comfortable. You can also see why it would be important to have a few thinking types on a committee made up mainly of feeling types. In each of the four categories, both types of people really need the other. There is something else very important about feeling types. Feeling types need harmony."

"Aha" number two for Jack. A lack of harmony distressed him, a feeling type. Yet some of his students, the thinking types, actually delighted in a good debate. Jack was identifying the source of some of the differences among him and his students. When he did not see eye to eye with his class, it wasn't that the students were being difficult; they were just being themselves.

Phil introduced the fourth category by asking how each person would prepare to write a paper. Many different styles surfaced. Phoebe wrote from an outline. Mark just jumped in and started putting down thoughts. Sarah liked to keep gathering more and more information on the topic and usually missed her own and others' deadlines. Laura kept neat little file folders for each aspect of the topic.

Phil explained how perceiving types are gifted with flexibility. When faced with a project, they gather much information and make continual adjustments to any plan previously compiled. Judging types possess the gift of organization. They are list makers, outliners, and are always concerned about closure.

"Closure!" That is what Jack felt it necessary to achieve each time he taught a lesson. Reaching the end, however, did not seem to matter to many of his students. Jack was not known for his flexibility. Maybe if he could become more flexible, he might be more open to the various tangents that inevitably touched and steered the class away from the week's lesson.

Phil answered a plethora of questions that night. No one was any more interested in the material than Jack. Laura's motive behind the educational event had been accomplished. Jack was about to embark on a long journey of understanding the personality-type differences among people. Even though Jack publicly displayed the most enthusiasm, every participant seemed to benefit from the time they had given to this event. For further reading, Phil recommended the book *Personality Type and Religious Leadership*, by Roy Oswald and Otto Kroeger,[1] for the professional church leaders and *God's Gifted People*, by Gary Harbaugh,[2] for the laity.

Past Application

I recently conducted a training seminar for a large church staff, disclosing the results of the MBTI to each person in a group setting. Like the fictitious Jack, many participants experienced multiple "ahas" throughout the meeting. "Much of the value of the MBTI," Lloyd Edwards states, "lies in the fact that people nearly always accept it as a valid self-description."[3] When I present MBTI results to a group, this understanding always surfaces: Two people may have great difficulty communicating just because each one is being him- or herself. People truly possess differing gifts. While I would never recommend using the MBTI as a criteria for calling pastors or staff members to a position, it can greatly enhance the ability of a team of professional church leaders, especially the newly hired, to communicate with one another. Indisputably, people have different needs, take in information differently, make decisions according to different criteria, and see the world from different perspectives.

When I hear a parishioner profile a professional church leader, the describer often states a strength of the leader and then follows it with a weakness at the other end of the same continuum. For instance, a person might greatly appreciate the depth and insight of a pastor's sermons, but also wish that pastor to be a little more sociable. Another may praise a staff person's ability to relate to a wide variety of people on a personal level while at the same time wishing the person were more objective. Church members may be more understanding of their leaders if they come to see that strengths and weaknesses are often connected.

Future Application

The MBTI is widely used in premarital counseling, team building, and self-understanding. A complete series of workshops is held annually on these and other topics associated with the MBTI. Some churches are starting to use the MBTI as they form various groups and task forces. In assembling a long-range planning committee, for instance, it would be very helpful to have both intuitives who could see the possibilities of the future and sensing types who would keep the feet of the committee firmly on solid ground. Thinking and feeling types both should be part of any major purchasing decision or building program in a church.

Lloyd Edwards presents a very interesting premise in his book, *How We Belong, Fight, and Pray*, calling for churches to work toward being "type-inclusive congregations."[4] Churches with a predominance of one personality type in their membership or leadership often send negative signals to people of a differing type, who may feel they are not being heard or welcomed into a congregation. It is not necessary for every event, sermon, or workshop to appeal to every personality type. Yet there ought to be continual acceptance of every type and, over the course of time, programming offered for a wide range of personalities.

Clearly the goal is to include all types of people. And a church might begin the process of becoming type-inclusive by trying to understand what type of congregation it is currently. In fact, discovering one's personality type can reveal valuable insights about how one reacts to change. Similar to Edwards, William Bridges's book, *The Character of Organizations*, applies the principles of the MBTI to organizations.[5] He compares organizational character to the grain in a piece of wood. Grains appear in varying colors, textures, and strengths, but each with its own purpose. His writings can help any organization, including a church, discover its unique character. Bridges suggests that it is possible for an organization to change its personality type over time. He cites several examples of modern companies attempting to change their personalities and images. If this is true, it may also be possible for churches to learn to attract a great diversity of people by adopting a more holistic programming approach.

While the MBTI is a very helpful tool in understanding differences, it cannot explain everything. People possessing the same four letters on the MBTI may still be very different in many ways. People seeking to understand one another should try to understand as much about the others' backgrounds as possible. A person's birthplace, birth order, ancestry, occupation, and travel experiences are all major contributors to her or his uniqueness. No two people have ever met the same people, traveled to the same places, or had the same experiences. "The truth is, we're products of everything, genes, environment, family, friends, trade winds, earthquakes, sunspots, schools, accidents, serendipity, etc."[6]

The goal for every church should be to discover and celebrate the diversity of its membership while providing all of the resources necessary for each individual to carry out the ministry of Jesus Christ. It is only through understanding another's gifts that we may appreciate his or her capacity for ministry.

Using This Chapter with a Small Group

1. Find someone in your area who can score and interpret the MBTI and ask that person to conduct a continuing education event for your small group. For assistance, write or phone the Center for Applications of Psychological Type (CAPT), 2815 NW Thirteenth Street, Suite 401, Gainesville, FL 32609, 1-800-777-2278.

2. As an alternative or in addition to the above, focus on characteristics that make each person unique: birthplace, birth order, ancestry, travel experiences, occupation, and so forth. The leader might group people according to similarities, such as those born first, second, only, or last in a family. Once divided, ask members of each subgroup to share similar experiences. Report similarities to the larger group when finished.

3. Tape a piece of newsprint, several feet long, on the wall to make a time line. As a group exercise, list dates, using the birth year of the oldest person present as the beginning date. Ask people to call out significant personal events corresponding with the dates. Events might include moving from one house to another, deaths, graduations, job changes, and marriages, as well as noteworthy national or world news items.

4. The aim of this session should be to discover what makes each person in your group unique.

CHAPTER V

The Coupling Theory:
Enhancing Stability and Creativity

The Scenario

Laura, minister of Christian education and music, left in a sullen mood
from the shortest church council meeting on record. How could someone possibly be upset about a brief, well-directed meeting? Laura preferred more substance to a meeting. Though she had wanted to say something to generate more discussion, at First Church the staff tried to let the
laity conduct the jobs they were asked to do. That included Hector, the
newly elected moderator who chaired the meetings of the church council, which consisted of the chairs of all the church committees.

Hector was born to organize. He had laid out an entirely new
structure for the council. He called it his "stream of discussion" for the
flow of ideas. Hector's plan called for every new idea to wind its way
through a series of channels. All ideas should flow from an individual to
a committee to the church council to the business meeting. Hector believed that the more groups that approved an idea, the more input and
refinement it would receive. Mark, the pastor, welcomed Hector's ideas.
Mark disliked taking charge of any organizing or restructuring effort and
depended on people like Hector to hold the reins.

Hector also announced at the church council meeting that every
church committee should become fully aware of what every other committee was doing. To accomplish this, every committee chair was asked
to submit a report in writing to the other members of the council. Since
his college days, Hector had never conducted a meeting without his little
buddy in hand, *Roberts' Rules of Order*. He prided himself on being a
veteran in the use of these rules and seldom made a mistake in their
application.

"That was unlike any meeting I have ever attended," Laura posed to Mark.

"Yes, it did seem to run smoothly," Mark replied.

"Smoothly?" Laura said wryly. "If it got any smoother, we all would have slid off the agenda. We didn't achieve anything. We approved the agenda, breezed through old and new business, passed around a bunch of written reports, voted on two or three trivial items by ballot, and synchronized our calendars. I liked the informal discussion, the devotional time, and the sharing that used to occur when Brenda ran the meetings."

"If Brenda were still running the meetings, you would not be heading home right now," Mark reminded Laura. "We used to talk about a lot of items that we did not need to talk about. A few times we might have come up with something important when we got off the subject, but we also wasted a lot of people's time."

"A few times when we brainstormed a topic that surfaced during the meeting, those brainstorming sessions turned into a ministry. For me, those 'connecting moments' made the other rambling worthwhile," Laura counteracted.

"I'm not sure everyone would share your nostalgic view," Mark said. "I suppose we did not accomplish much at this particular meeting, but I overheard Sarah remark that it all had been done very efficiently. You know I'm not an organizer, so I really admire someone like Hector who knows how to bring some structure to a group. After all, you can never have too much organization, can you?"

In reality, Mark, too, was uncomfortable with the amount of structure applied to the church council meeting, especially being a Myers-Briggs type ESFP. Yet Mark defended Hector, because he himself had often been criticized for his lack of organizational ability. Mark thought Hector's approach would help appease those who had asked for the meetings to be better organized. Even though Mark lacked any proficiency whatsoever with the bureaucratic model, he had "bought in" to this old paradigm. He was unable to see that many of the new ministries at their church had surfaced precisely as a result of their loose church council structure. A loose structure leads to more creativity.

Options

Many of our churches believe that more structure is always better. Many
have never paused to look for advantages that might be associated with a
looser structure. For years, institutions and churches have assumed "the
more the better" in terms of structure. How can you possibly have too
much organization in the church council or any committee, board, cell
group, task force, or ministry group? For many people "good organizing," like growth, love, enthusiasm, and unity, is an intangible that they
just cannot get enough of. Everyone wants to "tighten up" the structure,
especially when one deliberates on the alternative of "loosening up." It
just doesn't sound good for a church to "hang loose," "be at loose ends,"
or "run a meeting loosely." Many would argue that in this particular
scenario, Laura has no option except to endure Hector's tightening up of
the church council.

The Theory

Laura was not appeased after her conversation with Mark. She kept
repeating Mark's words, "You can never have too much organization,
can you?" *Was that statement really true? Could one create less structure without wasting people's time?* If anyone could assess the validity
of Mark's words, it would be Dr. Hastings.

"This is Laura Fisher calling for Dr. Hastings."

"Yes, this is Harold. Good to hear from you again. How are
things at First Church?"

"That probably depends on whom you ask," Laura said.

"Well, you are the only one I am talking to now. How are things?"
Harold asked again.

"Overall, fine," Laura explained. "But I am somewhat frustrated
with the new form the chair of our church council has devised for our
meetings."

Laura continued to explain all of the changes that Hector had
incorporated into the meetings and procedures. She also reported her
conversation with Mark and ended with Mark's summary, "It is impossible to have too much organization, isn't it?" That statement elicited a
response from Harold.

"Would you like to hear a little joke?"

"Sure," said Laura, "I could use one."

"This woman went to the doctor," Harold began. "When she arrived she noticed that the building contained two front doors. One door displayed a sign that said 'general' and the sign on the other door read 'specific.' Pondering the situation, she entered the door marked 'general,' where she was greeted by two more doors. Each of these doors also had a sign. One read 'physical' and the other, 'mental.' She quickly hurried through the 'physical' door. This time she was not surprised to discover two more doors, one marked 'surgical' and the other, 'therapeutic.' She proceeded through the 'therapeutic' door and discovered she was back out on the street. When she arrived home, her husband asked, 'Did you get help?' She replied, 'No, but they sure were organized.' " Harold chuckled more than Laura at the humor, but Laura got the message.

"It is possible to have too much organization and structure," Harold said. "Sometimes the amount of organization can actually detract from accomplishing the intended objectives. But people do not always respond well to the terms *less organization* and *less structure*. The best way to talk about these issues is to introduce the word *coupling* into our organizational theory vocabulary."

"Coupling?"

"Yes," continued Harold. "Coupling refers to the degree of interaction between two units, groups, or people within an organization. Coupling may be tight or loose. Certain areas of an organization may be tightly coupled and others loosely coupled. Thomas Peters and Robert Waterman, in their book *In Search of Excellence*, talk about simultaneous loose and tight coupling within an organization.[1] Karl Weick, however, was the first to suggest that an organization might want to loosely couple the elements that make up the organization.[2] Previous discussion regarding coupling had always assumed that organizations should tightly couple their elements."

"What exactly do you mean by tightly coupling the elements?" asked Laura.

"Tightly coupling the elements includes linking various committees, defining communication patterns, drawing up organizational charts, mailing out agendas, instituting interoffice memo procedures, and establishing chains of command."

"Okay," Laura responded, vaguely remembering seminary lectures about the bureaucratic model.

"The most fascinating part of the coupling theory," Harold continued, "is the discussion of the divergent effects [probable outcomes] that result from either tightly or loosely coupling the elements. Tight coupling leads to regularity, stability, predictability, control, and efficiency. Loose coupling leads to variability, innovativeness, creativity, empowerment, and effectiveness.

"I have never thought about it before your call today, but the church might be an excellent place to apply this theory. It would seem that the church needs stability and control in some areas and creativity and empowerment in others. From your discussion of your church council, you might have needed a little bit tighter coupling, which Hector was able to bring to its structure. But Hector's model might be quite dangerous if applied to other parts of the church where creativity is desired—such as the worship service and places where 'hands on' ministry takes place."

Laura thanked Harold for his time and insight. She had phoned to see what could be done about the church council meetings and had come away with a broad understanding of the reasons behind her frustrations, not only in the council meetings, but also in many groups within her church and denomination. Laura, a person who thrived on creativity and innovation, could see why she was so upset with the new changes that Hector had made.

She later recalled the personality-type differences between her and Mark—why they might have differing views of the situation; she was an intuitive type and Mark was a sensor. "Intuitives see the possibilities and sensing types adhere to the practical," she remembered the consultant, Phil, saying. It was in Mark's, but not Laura's, personality to appreciate the step-by-step flow of the meeting produced by the tight coupling. Still, she would try to accept the new changes while focusing her efforts in areas that could be more loosely coupled to produce innovative results.

There were several places in the church where Laura might encourage the group to enjoy the results of a more loosely coupled system. One group was discussing the sponsoring of a community no-smoking seminar. Another group had considered the possibility of starting a support group for abused women. Laura saw ministry as a place where loose coupling could have the most advantageous effects. New ministries often need innovation, creativity, and empowerment for those involved. At least for the time being, Laura would not make waves within the church council but, rather, give her energies and creative thoughts to those building new ministries within the community. Many small ministry groups would do well to avoid long agendas, organizational charts, and steering committees while emphasizing empowerment and creativity among members.

Past Application

In the church I pastor, I have tried to loosely couple areas directly related to ministry and tightly couple areas related to business. In our church of 275 active members, only three boards meet on a monthly basis. These boards are tightly coupled to one another, to the church leadership, and to a church council.

Within a month-long period, several other groups, task forces, and ad hoc committees may hold meetings. The other groups are usually designed to accomplish a specific and narrow task. Once that task is completed, they are dissolved. Task forces seldom report to anyone else, gain anyone else's approval, or ask for permission to deviate a little from the original plan. The original plan was usually their property anyway. It is amazing how much ministry can take place in this type of environment. It is discouraging to a committee to think that every detail must be approved before proceeding to the next ministry idea or domain.

I remember several years ago asking a church member why he appeared to be so frustrated after a day's work. He replied that he had spent two days waiting for a concrete inspector and had been unable to do anything until the inspector arrived. Although neither he nor I had a quick answer to solve the situation, we both knew something was wrong with the system where he worked. It probably had something to do with "coupling." Too often churches and other organizations have assumed that there is no way to control the coupling variable. But there are many ways to influence the interaction of organizational elements—once the leadership becomes aware of what those elements are. (See "Future Application," for an outline of categories of elements.)

If certain elements need to be tightened up within an organization, one may use many of Hector's techniques. On the other hand, if certain ministries, small groups, staff members, or volunteers need to be "freed up" to produce more creative and innovative results, then these groups or people must be "cut loose" from some of the structures.

For example, a new ministry may not need to go through all of the traditional channels of approval that task forces and committees have gone through in the past. If the leader of a new ministry must report every idea or direction to another group for approval, this will limit the number of creative ideas the group allows to surface and consider. A ministry group or other entity may be loosely coupled simply by limiting the number of connections the group has with the rest of the business structure within the congregation. Sometimes a ministry group needs only minimal connection with the rest of the congregation; the chair talking informally over coffee with a staff member or pastor every three or four months may be sufficient.

You might loosely couple an individual or group by not telling the person or group what the finished product should look like and how to go about producing it. When a pastor asks a layperson to do something, the pastor often comes across as knowing exactly how the task should be accomplished. The layperson, who may have a better idea for how to accomplish the task, will usually hold back on his or her own ideas, once instructed in the art of "how-to" by the pastor, who is viewed as a professional.

Consider a new group formed to design a no-smoking seminar for the community. The group may be tightly coupled to the congregation if the group is told the purposes of the seminar, where the seminar should take place, the total budget figure for the project, and the hopeful outcomes for the project. In contrast, the group could be loosely coupled if the group is told, "We really do not have any idea how to go about this. But someone had an idea to put on a no-smoking seminar for the community, and we got some of you together because of your gifts and skills in organizing and creativity. We appreciate your positive response when asked to be a part of this group, and we will be praying for your success." Undoubtedly, the latter group will design a more creative seminar than the first, not just because group members were less limited from the beginning, but because loose coupling leads to a more creative atmosphere within a group.

William James once said, "Genius means little more than the faculty of perceiving in an unhabitual way." Loosely coupling groups within the church runs counter to the traditional way of organizing. Loose coupling may be one of the most ingenious ideas of our day precisely for that reason.

Future Application

The coupling of any two elements within an organization may be studied or influenced. Only after understanding the elements that exist in an organization can a leader of that organization tightly or loosely couple those elements. Terry Astuto and David Clark have compiled a list of elements within an organization for the purpose of aiding organizations in studying coupling interactions.[3] I present a brief outline of these elements to help the reader explore additional areas where the coupling variable may be influenced.

Edificial elements are the formally recognized or designated components—the building blocks—of an organization. Every organization is built around certain types of units known as edificial elements. In a church these elements include the worship services, Sunday school classes, cell groups, positions, policies, and mission statement.

Functional elements are those things the organization intends to do. They come in two types, substantive and maintenance. Substantive functional elements in a church include gathering, worshipping, serving, evangelizing, and discipling. Maintenance functional elements include planning, calling pastors and staff, budgeting, and nominating.

Procedural elements are the processes an organization chooses to carry out its functions. These include personal decision making, needs assessment, feasibility studies, voting, discussions, surveying, and many other procedures.

Extraorganizational elements make up the fourth category. These are elements outside the church that interact with it in some way. These elements may include groups that meet in the church building, other churches in the denomination or community, other pastors, and heads of social agencies.

The final category is *idiographic* elements, the interaction between the unique people who make up an organization and their environment. These are the elements of human nature. Idiographic elements are the activities or ways in which individuals within the organization respond to organizational happenings. They include conversations, power blocks, and sense making.

Any two elements within an organization may be tightly or loosely coupled. The theory is as important for use as a discovery tool as it is for influencing outcomes. By analyzing various elements within the church, one may begin to see why certain areas seem "rigid" while others may appear to be "out of control."

Some people, like Laura, function better in loosely coupled environments, while others function more effectively in tightly coupled environments. When loosely coupled areas of the church are discovered, the church might want to make sure that the "right persons with the right stuff" are working in those areas to enhance creative ministry.

Using This Chapter with a Small Group

1.   Refer to the descriptive list of elements in the "Future Application" section. Discuss additional examples for each category listed, especially examples that apply to your own church. This is a good analysis exercise for a church, even if the coupling variable is not included in the discussion.

2.   On a chalkboard or newsprint, place the headings "tightly coupled" and "loosely coupled" at the top of two separate columns. Place the probable outcomes (listed in the "Theory" section of the chapter) directly under the heading for each column. Then draw a horizontal line under the outcomes. (See example, below.)

    Choose one of the elements of your church (listed in step 1, above). Is that element loosely coupled to other elements within your church? If so, list it in the "loosely coupled" column. Is that item tightly coupled to other elements within your church? If so, list it in the "tightly coupled" column. Continue by listing other elements from step 1 in one of the two columns.

Tightly Coupled	**Loosely Coupled**
(Regularity, Stability, Predictability, Control, Efficiency)	(Variability, Innovativeness, Creativity, Empowerment Effectiveness)
Elements in the church	Elements in the church

3.   Review each item listed. Place a check mark beside any item that does not appear to be in the correct column based on the discrepancy between your desired outcome for that item and the probable outcome as listed at the top of the column.

4.   Brainstorm possible ways to change the coupling factor for the items checked.

CHAPTER VI

Plank's Constant:
God Is at Work in the World

The Scenario

Harold Hastings had done a lot for First Church. As a token of her appreciation, Phoebe offered to buy Harold lunch. She promised that she would not "talk shop."

"Thank you for taking me to lunch, Phoebe," remarked Dr. Hastings. "It really wasn't necessary. It has been very gratifying to see how you've used the organizational theory material in your church. I love to see people put legs on theories and walk them through. An untested and unapplied theory benefits no one except its conceivers. I have appreciated the opportunity to offer some suggestions.

"For some reason, I have never really been tapped as a resource in my own church. Oh, I'm asked to do traditional tasks like everyone else, but no one there has ever picked my brain, as you people have."

"I can't understand that," offered Phoebe.

Harold suggested, "I believe Jesus' insights carried more weight outside of his home town. Maybe there is a similar principle at work here."

"We certainly appreciate all that you have done for us," said Phoebe. "Laura, Mark, I—and others—want you to know how much we value your wisdom in the area of organizations. I think God wanted us to bump into each other that day in the mall."

"I'm certain of that, too," replied Harold. "I believe strongly that God works in our daily lives."

"Mark preached a sermon about that last Sunday," said Phoebe. "He suggested that God is working simultaneously in more than one person's life to accomplish something. He used the text of Peter and Cornelius and approached it from the standpoint of dual visions from God. It was a creative sermon. Some in our congregation may not believe that God works in ways as earthy and dramatic as Mark suggested, but I do. I am convinced that God uses a variety of methods to accomplish desired purposes."

"Can God work even through organizational theorists, Phoebe?" questioned Harold.

"Especially organizational theorists," Phoebe assured him.

"I like your pastor," said Harold. "I am pleased to hear that he feels that way about the workings of God. A couple of fellow professors at the college are working on a project about the kingdom of God—how God is at work in the world. They have discovered that physicists can actually teach theologians something about how God works. They are two very unlikely research partners, but if you get a chance to hear their work, you might find it fascinating."

"Any chance of that happening?" Phoebe suddenly remembered that she had promised not to talk about business over lunch, but she was not about to remind Harold of that now. She had experienced some renewal in her life and welcomed the opportunity to explore more in depth how God works in her life.

"Yes, I'm sure there is a chance of it," Harold answered. "You ought to know by now that professors love to talk about their work, especially to interested parties. If you are serious, I'll see what I can do about arranging a meeting for you with one of them."

"Wonderful."

Phoebe and Harold talked about a host of other issues before saying good-bye. The next day Harold phoned Phoebe to let her know that he'd scheduled her an appointment with Dr. Westberg. After he hung up, Phoebe realized that she did not even know what subject Dr. Westberg taught. She would just have to discover that when she met him.

Options

This chapter will explore the kingdom of God in a fresh, new way. For too long people have equated the kingdom of God with the church. While Christians often praise God for the creation, few ponder more deeply how our God might be at work throughout the creation. The scientific community has made many breakthroughs that suggest that God is very much at work in the creation, even at the most elemental levels of the universe.

The community outside the church is changing. Christians are starting to view society as hostile or at best indifferent to the church. While many churches have successfully reached out to their communities, the risks of community ministry increase as the community outside the congregation becomes more hostile. For more of the people of God to gain the necessary courage to reach out in a changing world, they must view the kingdom of God as broader than the walls of the church. They must realize that God is already at work in the world. This chapter challenges the assumption that the kingdom of God is contained within the church of God. It also challenges the assumption that science and religion are incompatible.

The Theory

Phoebe had grown quite comfortable with the company of Dr. Hastings and had forgotten how intimidated she could feel inside a professor's office.

"Come right in," offered Dr. Westberg. Phoebe entered and surveyed the scene. Books everywhere. Not a sign of paint or wallpaper. Many of the book spines included the word physics. Surely Dr. Hastings had not sent Phoebe to a physics professor. *Physics?*

The shrill thought sent chills down Phoebe's spine. She could remember only one physics professor at college, and her memory of him was not pleasant.

"You're a physics professor?" Phoebe managed to say aloud, in a give-away tone.

"Yes," Dr. Westberg said with a chuckle, "but don't let that scare you. A few of us are quite normal."

"I'm sure you are," Phoebe said unconvincingly.

"Harold said you are interested in hearing about some of our research. How much do you know about quantum physics?"

Phoebe's blank stare and shrug responded for her. She was

beginning to feel like she was in the middle of an episode of the "Twilight Zone." What in the world could a physics professor have to say about the kingdom of God? Yet . . . this had to be the right place. She would give Dr. Westberg five minutes to mention the kingdom of God. If not, she'd politely excuse herself.

"I'll start somewhere near the beginning," Dr. Westberg said after noting Phoebe's expression. "At the turn of this century, Max Plank made a breakthrough in his study of black-body radiation."

"Black-body radiation?" Phoebe quizzed. Now she knew she was in the twilight zone.

"Yes," said Dr. Westberg. "Some types of metal exhibit a tone close to the black end of the color spectrum when cool. Plank discovered that one of these metals displayed a very unusual characteristic. Once heated, it changed from black to red to white with none of the traditionally expected colors interrupting the cycle. Think about a prism, Phoebe."

"Yes, okay," she replied. "A prism normally displays several colors, more than just black, red, and white."

"Exactly," said Dr. Westberg. "If light is a wave, then any material that changes color—from one end of the color spectrum to the other —should show every color that we normally see in a prism. Prior to Plank, physicists had viewed light as a wave, but they could not use wave theory to explain what occurred in black-body radiation. Plank suggested that light consists of packets, or particles of energy, rather than a wave and devised what is called Plank's constant, which modified Wein's earlier formula, to accommodate for the discontinuous nature of the energy packets."[1]

"By discontinuous, you mean changing from black to red to white while skipping the other colors," Phoebe offered her own clarification.

"Yes," replied Dr. Westberg. "Plank discovered an unidentifiable force in nature that maintains a separation between packets of energy. Physicists could not describe, view, or catalog the force, but they could measure it. Plank talked of 'another world of reality behind the world of the senses: a world that has existence independent of man.'[2]

"Because scientists could not describe the force, it took about twenty-five years for them to make much progress in studying it. Werner Heisenberg, in 1925, studied particles of light strictly by their function, rather than as an entity, and coined the phenomena the 'uncertainty principle.'[3] About that same time, Max Born showed that scientists can predict only with probabilities, not certainties, how particles will react when subjected to outside influence. Scientists had never before used the word *probability* to describe anything in the physical world. Up to that time, physicists believed that the elemental parts of the world behaved with certainty when subjected to the same conditions.

"Heisenberg studied at the Neil Bohr Institute. Bohr introduced the theory of complementarity, which said that any observer will change a particle—just by studying it; in studying the wave of a particle, the observer must alter the nature of the particle. With their research, Bohr and Heisenberg shattered the principle of determinacy on which all science had been based up until this century."

Five minutes were up. Dr. Westberg had still not mentioned the kingdom of God. But this was interesting stuff. "Stuff" was not a term Phoebe would use in an intellectual quest, but it was the only term she could think of to describe what Dr. Westberg was explaining.

Dr. Westberg went on, "Scientists have continued to discover the effects of an 'unexplainable presence' at work on particles at the subatomic level. This force allows particles to make decisions. 'Particles appear to make decisions based on decisions made by other particles.'[4] This unexplainable force also produces a tunneling effect.[5] In certain instances, particles seem to appear and disappear out of nowhere, going through what were constructed to be impervious boundaries by way of seemingly invisible tunnels. This force also causes identical particles to behave differently according to the shape of the space around them. Particles seem to have a mind of their own.

"I have been busy trying to discover the current research being done regarding this unidentifiable force. Dr. Granger has been busy trying to discover its application to the kingdom of God."

There was the phrase Phoebe had waited to hear.

"There indeed seem to be connections," Dr. Westberg suggested. "Theologians study God in much the same way that physicists study this unidentifiable force: by its function and effect on other things. If this unidentifiable force is not God, it at least can provide an analogy for studying God. Modern physics has opened the doors of science to the unexplainable. The more scientists study particles, the less they can predict about particles. As a physicist, I would be the last person to argue that God cannot work to change the laws of nature. In fact, the laws of nature appear to be guidelines constantly susceptible to outside influence. . . If you'd like, I'd be happy to set up an appointment for you to talk further about these matters with Dr. Granger."

"Yes," said Phoebe. Overwhelmed, it was all she could find to say. She was tempted to ask for some sources from Dr. Westberg but quickly decided to leave well enough alone. Amazingly, she seemed to have captured some of what he was trying to say, although she hoped he would not give her a quiz. She wasn't sure she would be able to recall any of the details, but she was able to construct parts of a very big picture. She was beginning to understand that some scientists believe that God is at work in our world in very unusual ways.

"In fact," said Dr. Westberg, "I'll see if Dr. Granger is in now." Phoebe wasn't sure she could absorb any more information today, but these people were being very gracious and she wanted to accommodate them. Dr. Westberg made the call. "Dr. Granger said he has some time if you would like to stop by his office. It is number 312 in Recitation Hall."

"So you have already been to see my colleague, Dr. Westberg," Dr. Granger said to Phoebe. "It might have been better if you had talked to me first. Dr. Westberg has a way of jumping right in and assuming that his listeners have the same swimming skills in physics that he has. Were you able to decipher any of the vernacular?"

"I think I understood where he was trying to go with it. He kept talking of this unidentifiable force in nature."

"That is correct," Dr. Granger responded. "Physicists have opened the door to God. The problem is that the average church member still sees science and religion as incompatible. Christians are actually suffering from an outdated perspective on the world. Christians have often felt a gap between God and themselves. Occasionally the gap is bridged by a mysterious presence of God. But with no language to talk about this presence, they dismiss it as a mystical experience. The Ulanovs say that 'gaps should not lead to losses, but to openings.'[6] Modern science has opened the gap from us to God.

"The kingdom of God has been discussed ever since the incarnation of Jesus Christ. Somewhere along the way, Christians began thinking that the kingdom of God meant 'church.' Norman Perrin suggests that equating the kingdom of God with God's church came about when people began to view the kingdom of God as a concept rather than a symbol.[7]

"This began to change in the late 1800s when Johannes Weiss suggested that the kingdom of God was 'a divine storm which was to break out in order to destroy and to renew the world.'[8] Later, Bultmann spoke of the kingdom of God as the critical choice to be made by a believer in deciding how to relate to God. Although still conceptual, Weiss and Bultmann began to move other theorists away from likening the kingdom of God to the church. C. H. Dodd broke entirely from the conceptual when he suggested in 1935 that the kingdom of God be interpreted through the symbols contained in the parables. The parables then surfaced as a rich and sundry background for relating the kingdom of God to daily living.

"Liderbach suggests that the kingdom of God is a tensive as opposed to a steno symbol.[9] Steno symbols indicate a distinct referent in a one-to-one correlation. Tensive symbols can never be confined to any one referent or even an assortment of referents. The kingdom of God as a tensive symbol suggests that there may be as many different interpretations of how God is at work in the world as there are people in the world.

"Dr. Westberg's readings and findings have complemented this view of the kingdom of God. Many take comfort in hearing a physicist talk of an unidentifiable presence in the world—it confirms and helps explain a wide assortment of happenings that are otherwise unexplainable. According to Morton Kelsey, since New Testament times, people have had five types of spiritual experience:[10] direct action of God through healings and miracles; indirect revelations through dreams, visions, and inward hearings; intuitive discernment; direct knowledge apart from the senses; and direct possession in the form of prophecy, tongues, and interpretation of tongues.

"While the tendency was there to attribute mysterious happenings to the work of God, the individual felt he or she might be ridiculed, especially by those who believed that experience has meaning only if it can be verified by the senses. With the advent of modern physics, science has become open to the unexplainable. Church members just do not realize it yet. Dr. Westberg and I hope to change all that. The goal of our work is to free people to talk about how God is personally at work in their lives. By getting the word out, we hope to hear of many people's encounters with God."

Dr. Granger had helped Phoebe apply Dr. Westberg's research. While she had not grasped many details or illustrations, she understood the passion behind their work. She too had often felt a mysterious presence in her life which she wanted to attribute to God. The work of these two professors would give her courage to talk more openly about her experiences.

In his Sunday sermon Mark had suggested that God works through various people when accomplishing a task. It appeared to Phoebe that God had been hard at work with physicists, theologians, and theorists to renew in the church an understanding of the presence of God in the world. Phoebe was more convinced than ever that God was guiding her life and the life of First Church.

Past Application

I have had the opportunity to ask several small groups: "Have you ever had a mystical experience?" The results have been amazing. People readily begin to discuss extraordinary ways in which God has influenced their lives. Some have received messages from God. Others have had premonitions that have come true. Others have found meaning through dreams. Nearly every person I have ever asked has had what she or he would term a mystical experience.

Yet very few people choose to discuss their experiences without prompting. Some in the small groups say, "Now, I have never discussed this with anyone." I wonder why? One possibility is that Christians still view their mystical experiences as incompatible with the most respected intellectuals of our day, the scientists. Christians need to hear that many scientists would no longer scoff at their experiences. If God is regularly at work in our lives in mysterious ways, then we, as Christians, should tell others what we believe God is doing. I believe that we are moving in a direction that makes science and religion increasingly harmonious. What a pleasant thought.

Future Application

Many authors have written of the changing role of the church. Loren Mead suggests that Christians are shifting toward a third paradigm in the history of the church.[11] He equates the first paradigm with the early church years, when the world was seen as hostile toward the church. The second paradigm occurred when the world was viewed as synonymous with the church. For many centuries, the pope and the emperor were equal and congenial with each other in their power holdings. During that time the pope crowned each emperor. Napoleon was the first to snatch the crown away from Pope Pius VII, in 1804, and place it on his own head. For years the church has been progressing toward a third paradigm, where once again the world is seen as distinct from local churches, and the church as distinct from the world. And yet God is very much at work in that world. Scientists who convince Christians that God is already at work in their world will empower those Christians to minister more fully to the world around them.

Mead encourages church members to view ministry possibilities and opportunities as beginning at the doors of the church.[12] Kennon Callahan encourages pastors and church members to view the territory beyond the church walls as a mission field.[13] If the church is to reach out into an incompatible and sometimes antagonistic world, Christians must be given the comfort of knowing that the presence of God will go with them. Ministering to neighborhoods and communities must be coupled with an understanding of the kingdom of God at work beyond the walls of the church. Christians need encouragement to reach out. They also need the comfort of knowing that God will go with them and work with them in remarkable ways. Jesus has said, "Go therefore and make disciples of all nations. . . . And remember, I am with you always, to the end of the age" (Matt. 28:19-20).

Using This Chapter with a Small Group

1. Begin by asking people to define the kingdom of God. Do people equate the church with the boundaries of the kingdom of God? Or do they view the boundaries of God's kingdom as limitless?

2. Ask the group this question: Have you ever had a mystical experience? Many might share specific encounters if given adequate time. Do not try to define mystical experience. Allow each person to do so individually. Some may wish to share experiences of friends or family members.

3. Discuss how the world views mystical experiences.

4. Discuss how modern scientists well acquainted with quantum physics might view mystical experiences.

5. Discuss ways that people might open themselves to a view of the kingdom of God at work in the world.

CHAPTER VII

Goals or Constraints:
Why Do You Come to Church?

The Scenario

Phoebe had several reasons to go the mall—to pick up a couple of thank-you cards, drop off some shoes to be repaired—and ponder a new issue. The mall always lent itself to the exploration of ideas. The walking abetted her reflection. The particular problem on her mind was not exactly her responsibility, but Phoebe had become dedicated to doing everything she could to help First Church run smoothly so it could better accomplish its mission. As she walked, she remembered the time she had bumped into Harold in the bookstore several months ago. As she pondered her problem, she realized how much Harold would be able to help.

"Harold!" Phoebe exclaimed. "I was just thinking about you."

"Well, that must mean you have a new problem to discuss regarding your church," Harold formulated.

"How did you ever guess?"

"What's on your mind?" Harold asked.

Phoebe started right in. "A few months ago at a joint meeting of Sunday school teachers and members of the board of Christian education, Mark announced that he would like to begin promoting evangelism through the Sunday school classes. He talked about how the Sunday school class has traditionally been the outreach arm of the church. Mark had done some thinking about where our church had come in recent years and where God might be leading us in the near future. For several reasons Mark believes that it is time to make evangelism our major emphasis. He stated his case for evangelism very persuasively. In fact, everyone in the meeting agreed with him.

"Everyone agreed. But in the last few months nothing has happened. Mark assumed that with a topic like evangelism and a target like the Sunday school classes, we would see some results. He had a well-planned presentation, but absolutely nothing has transpired since the original meeting. I can't figure out what went wrong."

"Yes, I think I have some material well suited for this problem," Harold said. "Give me a few days to gather some of my notes, and then I could meet with you next week."

"How about lunch?" Phoebe offered.

"That would be fine," replied Harold.

Options

Evangelism results can indeed be realized through the Sunday school program. Some churches have successfully split Sunday school classes when they reached a certain attendance mark and continued to grow. Other evidence suggests that Sunday school attendance can be more easily increased by adding new classes rather than working through existing classes. Certain churches start a new Sunday school class every two to four years.

Someone might suggest that Mark got off on the wrong foot by announcing his evangelism program to the wrong group. He might have promoted evangelism through the cell groups, the worship services, or the Bible studies. Many churches have experienced dramatic growth through cell groups.

As another option, Mark may have emphasized an invitational approach to evangelism where people are asked to invite friends to Sunday school and church. Many churches have given awards for inviting the most friends to Sunday school. Some churches have found success in contests that promote percentage increases in the overall Sunday school program.

Another option might have been to add an additional worship service. Some churches add a second Sunday morning worship service during the summer months. Others offer a second service year-round. Still others have successfully offered a differently styled worship service on Friday or Saturday night. Some churches have even targeted families with a Sunday afternoon worship service directed toward their needs and interests.

All of these are good suggestions. However, there is a fundamental reason why it is so difficult for a church to announce a goal or a program and then expect the membership to rally around that emphasis. No matter what approach Mark may have taken, very few results occur strictly by way of announcement.

Traditionally the church has depended a great deal on announcements. Just try to remove the announcements from worship services. It can be done, but rarely without warfare. Many people tacitly believe that every task in the church receives its inspiration from the Sunday morning announcements. On the surface, it seems to work. Someone announces an outing; people come. Why should we expect any less in Mark's announcement to the board of Christian education? The problem is that announcements seem to work only when the project directly coincides with the hearer's personal desires. Wait a minute. Am I suggesting that the work of evangelism is not a part of every church member's personal desire? Let's see what Harold has to say about this matter.

The Theory

"Hello, Phoebe," said Harold. "Have you been waiting long?"

"Not at all," Phoebe replied.

Phoebe and Harold chatted a few minutes. As the conversation flowed, Phoebe was hardly aware that Harold had turned the discussion to Mark's evangelism concern.

"What would you say are the major goals of your church?" asked Harold.

"Teaching people about God," Phoebe started, "helping them to grow spiritually, meeting needs within the community, the state, and our world through mission giving, growing numerically."

She waited for a response. Hearing none, she continued contemplatively, "Speaking out on important issues, challenging people to see the other side of certain issues, helping people starting new ministries, and helping them grow in their role as ministers."

Harold asked for clarification on a few of the goals then asked, "Why do people come to First Church?"

"Companionship. They come to see their friends and to know that they belong to a community of believers," Phoebe said without hesitation.

"The cell group provides that for me. I'm sure others find a sense of fellowship within their Sunday school class or a particular board or committee. When people work on a project, they seem to enjoy the camaraderie. The task is sometimes secondary. I also come for help in making sense out of life. The messages from Mark and my friends help with that."

"The church is really not different from any other organization," said Harold.

"What do you mean?"

"Well, the reasons people have for belonging to organizations almost never match the goals of the organization."

Phoebe quickly recalled some of her declared goals for First Church. Harold was right. There was no connection between the goals and her second list of why people came to First Church.

"I wonder if my perception about our church is unique?" Phoebe thought aloud. "I wonder if other churches would be different?"

"Probably not," replied Harold. "People in organizations often join for reasons other than the stated goals. Most organizations possess a raison d'etre, which is seldom, if ever, the motivating factor in the members' attendance or recruitment."

Frustrated, Phoebe replied, "But I have often heard our pastor, even denominational leaders, say, 'Our mission is what binds us together. It is the glue of our organization.' They might come unglued if they heard this conversation!"

"I'm sure your church, and mine, was founded on mission concerns," said Harold, "and mission is probably still the most appropriate reason stated why various churches and church members gather together. I am in no way suggesting that the goals of First Church, which you listed earlier, are not important. Each one sounded like a very worthwhile pursuit. Even though the mission of the church is not the primary reason people attend, without it, there would be no church. Preaching about goals and promoting a vision of the future for the church are beneficial tasks. But the church must do more than announce a goal if it expects the goal to be carried out. Over the years the goals of an organization, and even the various missions of a church, become more like constraints than goals."

"What do you mean by constraints?" Phoebe asked.

"Restrictions. Things we feel forced or compelled to do. Normally we think of goals quite differently, as things that motivate us. In

1964 Herbert Simon suggested that organizations possess constraints rather than goals and that goals had little to do with membership motivation or with organizational decision making.[1] Simon said, `We discovered that it is doubtful whether decisions are generally directed toward achieving a goal. It is easier, and clearer, to view decisions as being concerned with discovering courses of action that satisfy a whole set of constraints.'[2]

"A few people in church may be motivated to action by the mere announcement of a large-scale evangelism campaign. After all, Simon also said, 'One person's goals may be another person's constraints,'[3] but for the vast majority of parishioners, evangelism is more of a constraint than a motivating factor."

"If this guy figured this out thirty years ago, why haven't more people picked up on it?" Phoebe asked curiously.

"How do you think people would react if Mark stood up Sunday morning and said, 'I realize that evangelism, discipleship, and ministering to others have very little to do with why you attend First Church.' "

"I see your point," Phoebe replied.

"It isn't necessary to advertise and explain to the masses every strategy or theory that church leadership understands and chooses to carry through on," Harold continued. "But once the leadership understands the goals and constraints dilemma, they can better motivate people within the organization to accomplish its mission. To carry out this theory, the first thing you should do is forget about motivating people in the organization by way of pronouncements. William Quinn suggests, 'CEO's avoid the pronouncement of goals because they tend to centralize the organization.'[4] And in a church, without the controls or incentives of business, centralizing mission can be deadly."

"That is what happened to Mark," Phoebe said.

"Probably so," Harold concurred.

"Phoebe, you could make a presentation to the board of Christian education similar to the format I used with you," Harold suggested. "The presentation could be even more dramatic and convincing with visual aids. I would surmise that the group could come up with quite an extensive list of goals for which the church should be involved. I would print each goal on a board or newsprint, allowing the discussion to carry on as long as possible. Even with a long list of goals, I would also guess that, just like yourself, very few of the reasons that motivate them to come to church would be contained in the list."

Harold could see the wheels turning. He was not only an excellent teacher; he had also developed leadership skills within his students. As a college student Phoebe had never really burgeoned. But now she had truly cultivated her interests and abilities regarding organizational theory. Harold believed it was time for Phoebe to take the next step in educating others about organizational insights and theories.

Phoebe nodded, affirming Harold's suggestion.

"That's great," said Harold. "I know you can do it."

Phoebe continued to gather her thoughts about the presentation.

"Have you ever thought of going back to graduate school?" inquired Harold. He thought he would offer a dare.

"No, that was never one of my personal goals," said Phoebe. After a few moments of thought, she added, "I might be interested in taking a class or two in your field."

"You really seem to have a knack for this," said Harold. "I believe you would benefit from some continuing education in this area. Why don't we have a standing appointment for lunch? We could pursue this issue further and talk about any problems or dilemmas at First Church. It would give me a chance to talk through applications for some of the material I read."

"I would really like that," answered Phoebe.

"Let's say the first Thursday of every month, right here."

"Sounds good to me."

Past Application

I presented this theory during a seminar, in a format similar to the one Harold suggested to Phoebe. Participants compiled a very long list of goals for their respective churches, and I listed each goal on the board. Although the participants represented churches of different locations and sizes, it was amazing how similar their stated goals were, including evangelism, social action, glorifying God, discipling new Christians, reaching out to the homeless, giving to the poor, visiting the sick, being God's presence in the world, standing up for what is right, praying for others, ministering to everyone, and reaching out to the community.

I then drew a long vertical line and turned the discussion to a list of reasons people have for coming to church. I wrote down "worship, praise God, fellowship, child care, openness, somewhere to belong, meet new people, 'the right thing to do,' challenge one another to grow in the Lord, acceptance, fulfillment, music, learn more about God." As you can see, there were only two matches between the two lists: worship and learning about God. Often the stated goals of a church are very dissimilar to the reasons people join.

Future Application

The benefit of this theory lies more in its understanding than in its application. It is not so much a theory regarding a new approach as it is a theory for understanding why the traditional approach of pronouncements seldom produces results. By using and becoming frustrated with pronouncements, some pastors have experienced a sense of disappointment over the type of congregations they pastor.

Pastors lament: "I announced a visitation night the second Tuesday of each month and only two people have shown up. Doesn't this church believe in evangelism?" This theory should help remove some of that discouragement. All churches and organizations possess motivating factors that differ from their stated goals. It does not mean that the goals are not worthwhile. It does mean that the church will have to find a new way to motivate people to accomplish the mission of the church.

There are very good ways to motivate people to perform tasks related to the stated goals of an organization. Some will be discussed in chapter 10, when Phoebe is asked to chair the board of deacons.

Using This Chapter with a Small Group

1. Do the exercise presented in this chapter. List the goals of your church. Then list the reasons why you belong and compare the results. Are your church's goals different from its motivating factors?

2. Does your church use announcements? Do they use pronouncements? What are the expectations of your pronouncements? Are the expectations too high?

3. What alternative strategies has your church tried to motivate its members to accomplish your church's mission?

CHAPTER VIII

Retrospective Rationality: Were There Ever Any Bad Old Days?

The Scenario

At her weekly cell group meeting with Sonia, Sarah, Daniel, Brenda, Clyde, and others, Phoebe innocently proposed, "I read the dedication stone on the church building the other day. We have an anniversary coming up in our church. Why don't we have an old-fashioned ice cream social?" She had just put an idea aboard a train that would race the group headlong down the tracks of nostalgia. This is a train with no brakes, an endless supply of coal, no means of guidance, and no way to get back to the future.

"That is a great idea," responded Brenda. She was the first to hop aboard the train. "It would be nice to relive some of the church outings we used to have."

"I remember one day in particular," Sonia related. "We had a Sunday school picnic. We must have had four hundred people present, all regular attenders. It was a wonderful day. Games, eating contests, kids' relays. And that picnic was not that many years ago."

"There is no reason why we shouldn't have that many in our Sunday school program now," Brenda declared. "People are just not as committed to church as they used to be. It is impossible to compete with TV, the Community Center, Nintendo, Super Nintendo, Super Colossal Nintendo, Super Colossal Gargantuan Nintendo . . . " (Brenda was getting carried away as she was prone to do) "and school athletics."

"I remember when the youth football team started scheduling Sunday morning games for Jeremy," Sarah said. "I really should have said something then, but I didn't."

"Why, I can even remember when all of the businesses in town would close at noon on Wednesday, just so people could get ready to go to prayer meeting that night," said Clyde, the oldest member of the cell group. Clyde lived for this type of discussion. He really wasn't that old but loved to talk about the "good old days" as if he had firsthand experience of each decade since the turn of the century. "Not that long ago we had to put chairs in the aisles for our Wednesday evening prayer meeting." Almost everyone present thought Clyde surely must have meant Sunday morning worship rather than prayer meeting, but no one was about to challenge him, and besides, they were all having too much fun "creatively recalling" the events themselves.

"I know the pastor has been pushing evangelism through the Sunday school classes," Brenda said. "In the good old days, we never even had to talk about evangelism or things like tithing. People just came to church because it was the thing to do. I don't know where we went wrong."

"We used to have more kids in church than adults," Clyde said convincingly. "Where are all the kids? When my wife and I were sponsors of the Young People's Union, we had a whole slew of kids. And we didn't even bribe or offer the kids the things you have to today to get them here. We just said we were going to have a singspiration, and they came."

"It wasn't too long ago when I was a youth; we would sing in other churches," Sarah remembered aloud. "What was that group called? The Joy Singers? Singing sure brought us to church. Pastor Larry would fire up the old bus and off we would go. The speedometer did not register over forty-five, and I'm not sure the bus did either. More than once we broke down. But I think that was the best fun I've ever had."

Clyde chimed in again, "I remember when you young people used to sit and chatter in the back of the church. People would fan themselves like crazy. No air conditioning in those days. I don't know which was louder, the paper fans from the mortuary or the chattering kids. Life was simpler. There was not as much to do. Yes, we had fun in those days."

What in the world just happened?! Phoebe wondered. How had all this discussion mushroomed from her simple suggestion to have a church picnic? Who could have predicted such a nostalgia trip over a simple question regarding the past? The answer? Nearly anyone who has been a member of a congregation for any length of time.

Options

Everyone who has ever led a congregation or pastored a church knows that church members love to talk about the "good old days." Have you ever stopped to consider that there are no "bad old days"?

Many pastors try to fight the remembrances of former pastors. In reality, if a pastor returned to one of his or her previous congregations after a number of years, he or she would probably have difficulty living up to his or her own image. People tend to enhance the memories of former pastors and leaders.

Sometimes the current pastor and leadership view the lofty recollections of former leadership as a threat to their new plans and visions for change. Every pastor entering a new parish witnesses certain congregational characteristics that need changing. But people do not like to change. To promote change pastors often lean too far to the priestly or too far to the prophetic side of a continuum. "On the one hand, you bless the status quo (priest). On the other hand, you blast it (prophet). The effect is the same, nothing changes."[1]

Pastors can make the mistake of believing every glorified detail they hear about the past and interpreting such comments as personal dissatisfaction with the present. Mark could feel this way about First Church, but probably once he has been gone from the scene for some time, First Church will hold a "glorified" discussion about him and his pastorate in the presence of the new pastor.

As for the good old days, do you think the people of First Church really enjoyed being crammed into a church building with no air conditioning? Do you think the youth enjoyed embarking on an outing not knowing whether their bus would return them safely? Did Clyde fancy the children chattering and paper fans frolicking? People tend to remember only the good.

The Theory

Charles Perrow carries the concept of people remembering only the good one step further in his discussion of "retrospective rationality."[2] He suggests that people plan backwards more than they plan forwards. A professor, Perrow describes a time when he forgot to order textbooks for the coming year. When asked why he had forgotten, he immediately began to construct a new world in which the error was made rational, "I got bored with that text . . . the price of textbooks is going out of sight, the students are better and don't need spoon-feeding, and [I've wanted to teach from] a few marvelous articles I have never had the room for before."[3] Whether those reasons were in the back of the professor's mind when he failed to order the textbooks is immaterial. Those reasons never surfaced until the professor was asked to offer an explanation of why he had not ordered the textbooks. When faced with the embarrassment of saying he simply forgot, he was able to offer a more appealing explanation. The reasons never surfaced until the need arose.

Skinner,[4] Garfinkel,[5] and Bem[6] have all suggested that meaning is retrospective rather than prospective. Humans have the power to think, even to reason, retrospectively. No one wants to admit that she or he has failed. Warren Bennis suggests that it is people's failures that get them to reflect on their experiences.[7] But after enough reflection, the magnitude of the failure dims. When faced with the alternatives of admitting failure to another or offering a plausible explanation, most will offer some sort of credible explanation. After offering it enough times, the person is unable to tell for sure whether the explanation was ever there prior to the event. Most people give themselves the benefit of the doubt and suggest that the reasons occurred prior to the event. Perrow says, "Why then do we think we are smarter than we are? The answer is because of our enormous desire to make sense of things, to find an order, to acknowledge a rationality."[8]

The discussion at Phoebe's church cell group meeting shows the enormous power of people to remember the good. Even when there is nothing good in the event being recalled, people possess the ability to create good and recall it as if it were originally there. This is a power that no one can battle. It is impossible to convince someone that the good old days were really not that good.

Past Application

I used to battle the good old days, but I have since dropped this impossible task. I discovered that I was not battling the good old days; I was battling people's filtered perceptions of the old days. People guard and care for their remembrances better than they guard their physical possessions.

Just as people like to talk about the good old days, they are gener-
ally willing to create more good memories with the current membership
and leadership.

Given the opportunity, people are willing to invest the same kind
of energy in the present. A grand and gloriously interpreted past never
precludes a congregation from experiencing an even brighter future.
Opportunities to lead a congregation in new ways surface by ministering
to all of the people and allowing each to use his or her specific gifts for
ministry. For the church to grow, the current leadership need not seek
out a whole new set of people who do not speak so nostalgically of the
good old days. People just need an opportunity to reflect on the past
before being asked to move forward into the future.

Future Application

Kennon Callahan suggests that all organizations have an interim status.
"They are for the moment, the day, the season. All structures are tem-
porary, intermittent, provisionary. Each structure has its day in the sun
and then is no more."[9] Very few churches, however, would agree with
this concept without being convinced by someone they know and respect. Sometimes it is impossible to move a church forward until the
membership is convinced that the leadership understands its history.
When a church believes that the current leadership has no comprehen-
sion of its complicated and celebrated past, it may block the leadership
from leading in new ways. But when a church realizes that the current
leadership has taken the necessary time and spent the appropriate energy
in discovering the history of the congregation, a kind of "permission" is
granted to lead the church in a new direction. Gaining permission to
move forward is sometimes more a matter of comprehending the past
than of promoting the future.

Much has been written recently in the area of visionary leadership.
I commend the authors in their promotion of a vision for the church.
Visions help unify and create new language to go along with new actions
taken and modeled by the leadership. But a church may refuse to see a
vision of the future if the leadership has not acknowledged that they
have seen a vision of the past.

An understanding of the church's past may be obtained through in-depth conversations, sometimes formal interviews, with various church members. Obtaining information about a church's past is never a difficulty. Celebrating the past is important for a church that wishes to celebrate its future.

Using This Chapter with a Small Group

1.   Make a timeline of your church from the combined corporate
      memory of your group's participants. Obtain a long piece of
      newsprint to cover the length of a wall. At the right side of the
      newsprint, mark today's date. At the left side, mark a date as far
      back in the life of your church as anyone in the group can remem-
      ber. Fill in the middle with important dates and events of the
      church, including mortgage burnings, pastorates, tenures of staff,
      retreats, themes, new ministries, and programs.

2.   Ask the group to guess average worship and Sunday school at-
      tendances over the years and overlay these guesses onto the chart.

3.   As an option, supplement the finished timeline with real data of
      average attendances, giving, and other available historical figures.
      Annual reports of the region, synod, district, diocese, and so forth
      are an excellent source for these figures. Compute real dollars for
      budget figures if desired. Compare actual figures to guesses.

4.   Invite others to view, comment, or build on the timeline.

5.   As an option, invite other church members to attend your group
      and reflect on the church's history.

CHAPTER IX

Antagonists: How to Keep One from Destroying a Church

The Scenario

"Mark, Dinah is on the phone," the church secretary paged him through the intercom. "She sounds really upset about something. She says it is urgent."

"Hello," Mark said cautiously. Dinah had been a thorn in his side for quite some time. It seemed that nothing he did pleased her. He had tried to spend a little extra time with her—to satisfy her constant complaining. From stories he'd heard, Mark had come to realize that she'd been in conflict with every previous pastor. This was nothing personal. He never looked forward to meeting with her, and this was an especially busy week. Yet he found time in his schedule and made an appointment with her for two the next afternoon.

At 1:30 the next day, someone knocked on Mark's office door. It was Dinah. She had a habit of showing up early, and he knew she would state the reason for her impatience.

"I know I am early, pastor, but this was just too important to wait any longer," Dinah began.

"Come right in," Mark said. "May I get you a cup of coffee?" Mark always tried to be extra nice to Dinah, hoping to kill her with kindness.

"No, thank you," she replied. "I guess you know why I am here."

"No. That wasn't clear to me."

"I am here regarding the games night fiasco held in the church last Saturday."

Dinah had struck a nerve. Mark was really proud of the first ever "games night" at First Church. Sixty people had shown up to play

games and enjoy one another's company. Some found new chess partners. Others played board games. The kids played Twister and had a
blast. People brought snacks and shared a wonderful evening in the
church basement.

"I don't recall seeing you at the games night last Saturday, Dinah."

"I most certainly was not there," she said. "I would never be a
part of such nonsense within the church. Have you read your Bible?
Jesus turned over the tables of the money changers in the temple. If
Jesus would have walked in and seen what you people were doing, we
would have witnessed the cleansing of the temple all over again."

"I really do not see what connection playing games has . . . "

"It has every connection. And all of the others think so, too."

"All of the others?" Mark said inquisitively.

"Yes, a lot of people feel the same way I do," Dinah said convincingly.

"I had no idea. You are certainly the first to express your concerns
to me."

"I guess I'm the only one with enough courage to stand up for
what is decent. You know, this is not the first time that I have been sort
of elected to be the spokesperson for those disgruntled with all of your
goings-on."

"Yes, but I thought we had resolved those other issues." Mark's
voice was full of hope.

"Oh, I listened to your explanations for why the kitchen was such
a mess when our mission circle needed to use it and your accounting for
why Joe was elected an officer of the church, even when I warned you
about his background. But your explanations never seem to resolve
anything."

"I am beginning to see that," Mark said.

"All I am saying is that Jesus would not have approved of the
carrying-on and poker playing and money changing hands in the church."

"I can assure you, Dinah, that no poker playing or money . . . "

"Well, I'm sure you were not able to be everywhere at the same
time the other night, were you?" Dinah retorted. "And I hear you have
already planned another so-called games night in two months."

"Yes, we are considering. . . . I will be happy to relay your concerns to one of the boards."

"I'm sure that won't be necessary," Dinah said. "No doubt, they
have already heard."

Options

James Glasse cites several reasons why conflict is so prevalent in
churches.[1] First, and obviously, no two human beings are alike; it is
human nature to come into conflict. He also points out that ancient
divisions persist among people, from language and cultural barriers to
religious conflicts. Interestingly, he also cites the Gospel as a reason for
conflict in churches. He quotes Matthew 10:4-6, "Do not think that I
have come to bring peace, but a sword . . . " and points out the tensions
present in many Gospel stories. Conflict is a part of life, and many who
view the church as a living organism believe that conflict is unavoidable
within the church.

There are a variety of approaches to handling conflict. Many who
deal with difficult people try to appease them by every means possible,
as did Mark. An interpretation of Romans 12:20-21 reveals that trouble
makers will feel as if burning coals have been dumped on their heads if
they are treated with kindness rather than retaliation.

Others, who do not possess Mark's patience, retaliate. Retaliation
seldom works, although it can be quite effective in releasing anger for
the moment. But the newly compounded problem produces even more
future anxiety. Although many church leaders have tried, it is difficult
to win a battle against someone causing conflict within a church. Even
if the leader wins a battle, it rarely means that the war has ended.

Still others approach conflicts from a win-win standpoint. Proponents of conflict management testify to many successes based on this
approach. The leaders of the two conflicting groups are gathered together in an effort to help them communicate. Sometimes they are asked
to list their most salient concerns and then proceed to bargain with one
another. Through the communication process each side often discovers
various misunderstandings. Working through these, one hopes both
sides will be able to view the conflict with new glasses.

I see this win-win approach as the best tack to take ninety-nine
percent of the time. Dinah and others, however, seem to fall in a class all
by themselves.

The Theory

Mark knew he needed help with this ongoing situation. He decided to
call Jan Cramer, pastor of the Methodist Church a few miles away. In
the last community ministerial meeting, Mark had listened to Jan report
on an "Antagonists in the Church" workshop she had attended through
the Academy of Parish Clergy. If anyone could be labeled an antagonist,
Mark believed it was Dinah.

"Hello, Mark, what can I do for you?" Jan greeted him when he
called her office.

"Plenty," Mark replied. "I have just suffered through a horren-
dous meeting with one of my parishioners. I remembered your report
about a workshop you had attended—about antagonists."

"Right," Jan said. "I go to the Academy of Parish Clergy confer-
ence every year, and this year's focus happened to be on 'Antagonists in
the Church.' After hearing the scoop I don't think I have any antagonists
in my current congregation, but if I did, I certainly would feel better
equipped to deal with them."

"I wish I could say the same thing. I cannot believe you don't
have any conflict in your church," Mark commented.

"Oh, I didn't say that I don't have any conflict," Jan corrected. "I
said I don't feel I currently have anyone who could be labeled an antagonist. Ken Haugk, the workshop leader . . . "z

"Ken Haugk?" Mark interrupted. "Isn't he the founder of
Stephen Ministries?"

"Yes, that's the guy," Jan replied. "He developed a workshop to
help churches struggling with antagonists because he had encountered so
many churches with people who had blocked the use of Stephen Ministries."

"I believe this parishioner could block any ministry emphasis in
our church," Mark related.

"Ken Haugk defined antagonists very narrowly," Jan continued,
"as 'individuals who, on the basis of non-substantive evidence, go out of
their way to make insatiable demands, usually attacking the person or
performance of others. These attacks . . . tear down rather than build up
and are frequently directed at those in a leadership capacity.'"[2]

"Are antagonists always antagonistic?" asked Mark.

"According to the workshop, they can be dormant," replied Jan, "but it is very difficult to get an antagonist to stop being antagonistic altogether. When the antagonist is not causing trouble within the church, he or she is often causing trouble in a business, service club, school, or some other place.

"When dealing with an antagonist, your goal is to diffuse the situation rather than appease or win against the person. You don't try to meet all the antagonist's demands. Once you meet one demand, others are sure to follow. By definition, a true antagonist is not after a peaceful situation."

"What can you do to make an antagonist dormant or diffuse the situation?" asked Mark.

"Try to build a unified front," said Jan. "And build in clear and appropriate communication patterns and advertise them to the congregation. Develop support among your staff and leadership."

"Say a little more about the unified front," Mark requested.

"An antagonist 's decision to enter into battle is not based on the chances of winning. The goal of an antagonist is to disrupt, not to win a battle. The basis of an antagonist's decision to fire (or not fire) the first shot is the potential for disruption. A unified front advertises to the antagonist that there is very little chance of causing dissension. There are several ways to build a unified front: Let your personnel committee know of the behavior of the antagonist. Never stoop to that person's level. Never avenge. Also do not tolerate backbiting or negative behavior among your leadership. When all this has been accomplished, you have created a situation in which the antagonist can be impartially disciplined. Don't allow any special exemptions for the antagonist. When the antagonist attacks, provide appropriate discipline."

"But she claims there are a lot of people who feel the same way she does about certain issues."

"Have you ever heard her name anyone?" asked Jan.

"Come to think of it, I haven't," replied Mark.

"That is one of the ploys Haugk described, the ploy of the 'countless others.'"

"How in the world do you discipline a church member?" Mark asked.

"It can be done," said Jan without hesitation. "I'm not sure I would recommend this in all situations, but I am aware of a church in another part of this state that restricted a person's attendance in the church to worship services. Also, the antagonist was not allowed to attend any committee or business meetings.

"I'm sorry, Mark. I have an appointment coming in. Haugk has a book titled *Antagonists in the Church*."

"I'll try to pick up a copy on my way home," said Mark. "And thank you for your time."

"Let me know how it turns out," remarked Jan, "and remember that I will be praying for you."

Past Application

Like Jan, I do not currently have a person exhibiting antagonistic behavior in my church. Our church may be blessed, or an antagonist may be dormant within the congregation, but I have attended Ken Haugk's workshops and now feel more qualified to deal with an antagonist should the situation arise. (In the past I have approached the dilemma similarly to Mark, with a totally wrong approach.)

In one particular church, I decided to spend more time with the individual who was displaying antagonistic behavior. But it seemed that the more time I spent with the person, the more the person found to complain about. I would close the conversation feeling satisfied that a situation had been resolved, only to discover later that something I said had been misinterpreted. I have now come to believe that many of the things I said were misinterpreted purposefully.

I have helped to resolve several conflicts in churches when the people involved truly desired reconciliation. The problem in dealing with an antagonist, however, is that the antagonist does not desire reconciliation. When this occurs, the leadership must attempt to resolve the situation according to a different set of criteria.

It sounds very unconventional to try to diffuse a situation rather than appease an individual. Diffusing a situation goes against the widely held assumption that every situation can be handled by a win-win strategy. The ultimate goal should be for the person causing trouble to find renewal in God and in the church. But the immediate goal is to keep the antagonist from destroying the church and its leadership. It doesn't make sense to try to appease one person while allowing him or her to drive away a host of other committed Christians.

Future Application

While I have not dealt with an antagonist in my local church situation, I have helped other ministers and executives develop successful strategies for dealing with antagonists. Based on these case studies, I have found merit in Haugk's approach.

Recently I have heard reports of several denominations having "antagonistic churches." Haugk described the rare case where a pastor may be the antagonist within a local church. His discussion on this matter related to what that local congregation could do to improve its dilemma. I can foresee an interesting discussion on how to approach the problem of an antagonistic church or pastor causing trouble for an entire diocese, district, or even denomination.

Using This Chapter with a Small Group

1. If this chapter is pertinent to your church's situation, I suggest purchasing a copy of Ken Haugk's book *Antagonists in the Church*. Chapter 8 lists several red flags to help identify antagonists. If your group feels that antagonists are blocking ministry within the church, conduct a separate study of the book using its complementary study guide.

CHAPTER X

Means and Ends: Adding Two More Factors to Get the Job Done

The Scenario

"Congratulations on your election to the board of deacons," Harold said to Phoebe as they met for their monthly luncheon meeting. "You have given a lot of leadership to that congregation in the past year."

"Thank you," Phoebe replied. "I appreciate all of your support and insight. I feel I have developed in so many intangible ways over the last year. As I began to explore my interests in the area of organizational theory and apply my learnings to the church, it seemed that I grew spiritually at the same time."

"Do you have any assignments yet in your new deacon role?"

"As a matter of fact I do," Phoebe replied. "I had hoped we could spend a little time discussing that today."

"I'm ready if you are," said Harold.

Phoebe had finally been convinced of Harold's unwavering interest and desire to discuss the application of various theories. She had gotten over her intimidation and the feeling that she was imposing every time she asked Harold a question. It made sense to Phoebe to donate time in the areas where her greatest strength lay, and she had come to believe that Harold held a similar view. Thinking along these lines had finally led Phoebe to agree to serve as a deacon; in this role she could put her strengths to use for the church.

"I have been asked to help devise a plan to promote spirituality among the deacons and eventually to the church membership," Phoebe announced. "I remember our discussion, some time ago, about Mark's announcement, asking the board of Christian education to promote evangelism. I know I can't announce the spiritual emphasis to the board or the church and wait for something to happen. Spiritual development may be as much of a constraint on the congregation as evangelism. Conceptually every member would probably agree with the aims of evangelism and spiritual development, but getting them to do something about it will be a different story. How do I approach a task like this?"

Options

To promote spiritual development Phoebe could take a number of approaches. Most will focus on two major components: common ends and common means, or goals and plans. In the traditional approach, church leadership assumes that everyone agrees with the aim of the project (common ends). A great amount of work is done devising a plan (common means) for all members initially involved in a program. The leadership assumes that every member in the original group and every member in every other group will be able to follow the devised plan in achieving the uniformly desired results.

Two-step common ends and common means approaches (or goals and plans techniques) can and have been successful. The problem is that they work only when there is very little diversity within the group and when the goal of the program is a motivating factor for the members of the group (see chapter 7). Harold will introduce Phoebe to two *additional* factors to consider when promoting a program: diverse ends and diverse means. He will also discuss a possible order for the four factors.

The Theory

"You are right on target with your analysis of the situation," Harold began. "Even though spiritual formation is probably more of a constraint than a motivating factor for church members, there is a way to approach this problem."

"I'm not surprised to hear you say that," Phoebe said. "I knew you would have some suggestions."

"The particular theory I am about to explain has to do with means and ends," Harold continued. "Like Mark with the evangelism emphasis, many people begin with the announcement of the desired ends and expect the means to follow.

"There are actually four different factors to consider when planning a program: diverse ends and diverse means, and common ends and common means.[1] Let me briefly explain each factor. Diverse ends deals with the reality that each person potentially involved in the program has a slightly different idea of what outcomes should be achieved. Some may consider personal advantages. Others may consider benefits related to the church. Still others may have in mind outcomes related to the community. Nearly every group of people will have a diverse set of ends in mind when starting a project."

Phoebe listened intently and offered an example to see if she and Harold were on the same track. "I remember when the building task force made their proposal for our church addition. The chairman reported that at the first meeting the committee of eight held eight completely different ideas of what the addition should look like. As I think about that now, I realize that each building idea probably reflected a different benefit or use. The chair went on to announce that they had eventually reached a consensus."

"Good example," Harold said. "You've become a practical theorist. I can see you are on track with me. Sometimes in a committee of eight, there will be even twelve or thirteen different preferred outcomes!"

Continuing on, Harold said, "The *diverse means* factor suggests that there are also a variety of ways to accomplish a certain program or emphasis. There will never be one way to do something, no matter how simple the task may seem."

"I can see that," said Phoebe.

"The third factor is *common ends*," Harold said. "This, unfortunately, is the place where most people try to start. Most people begin a project by assuming that everyone will be focused on the same desired outcome. While that is a characteristic that may surface as the project progresses, the leadership should never assume common ends from day one.

"The fourth factor is *common means*. This factor kicks in when the people involved in the program perform the same or a similar task together as a group. Ironically enough, sometimes a group never gets to this point.

"Now let's talk about one possible order for these four factors, aimed at accomplishing your emphasis. Where should you begin? With *diverse ends*. You should recognize, from the very beginning, that the board of deacons will have a variety of concerns and outcomes in mind related to spiritual development. At this point it's enough just to recognize that the diversity exists; I would not spend time discussing or analyzing the diversity of aims. In implementing a program, it is advantageous to cycle through these four factors more than once. The recognition of diverse ends should take place now. A discussion of diverse ends should take place way down the road.

"In terms of activity, the place to begin is with *common means*. Try to think of one activity that would enable each member of the board of deacons to develop spiritually."

"We could promote daily devotions," Phoebe said quickly. "We could buy a small devotional book for each member and encourage them all to focus on the same devotional theme for a period of time. Or we could . . . " Phoebe never seemed to have any difficulty with brainstorming.

Harold tried to interrupt Phoebe's flow of suggestions, "Decide on one of those activities. Then plan it, model it, and promote it to the deacon board. Keep the activity very simple. Don't start by announcing an entire program. Keep in mind, though, that you are only half-way through your strategic plan. Up to this point, all you have done is recognize that diverse ends exist and begin one common means activity. Many others have started with a similar approach, but ended too soon.

"If the activity is carefully chosen and goes well, the common means will lead to sn atmosphere of a common end. Whatever activity you choose will induce the feeling that a very specific aspect of it is important. For example, if you choose to promote a daily devotional time for each individual in the group, and each one takes part in the activity, many of them will rediscover the importance of a personal relationship with God. Several people performing a similar worthwhile activity will lead to a unified feeling among the group that the aim of the activity is also worthwhile. After a while, not too long, someone will probably say, 'This activity has really led to . . . ' and announce a common end for the group. Others will probably chime in and agree, with the stated aim or goal being accomplished by the common means of engaging in the same activity.

"In time, the common end will instigate diverse means. Someone in the group—maybe you—might suggest a better way to accomplish the common end. Someone else will adapt the activity to his or her liking. Others will find entirely new approaches.

"Naturally, these diverse means or exercises will give rise to a discussion of the diverse ends held by the group, bringing you back to the beginning of the strategic cycle. After the group has energetically performed an activity together—leading to spiritual development—encourage a group discussion of the great diversity of aims accomplished by spiritual activities. Don't have this type of discussion at the start of the overall emphasis because at that point one or two people may feel that the initial group activity does not reflect their particular interests and aims. Get the people involved in doing something as a group, then talk about it later.

"The entire success of the approach often depends on getting the people to commit to a single, focused activity as a group. Without that initial step, many programs fail. Others fail later because as the program progresses, diversity is not allowed. I don't think you will have any trouble coming up with a single 'spiritual' activity for every member of your board to participate in. Brainstorming comes easily to you. If they try to focus on diverse ends when you announce the activity, steer them away from that discussion and try to get them all to commit to the initial activity. Then progress through the rest of the steps. And keep me informed, so we can make adjustments as needed along the way. I know you can do this task. Those who assigned it to you must think so, too."

Past Application

Several years ago I announced that I would hold a seminar for anyone wishing to discover his or her spiritual gifts. The project was very successful, but only for a limited number of people. The twenty who attended each week were the same twenty who would probably have shown up no matter what the seminar topic. I had begun by assuming the discovery of one's spiritual gifts to be a motivating factor, when in reality it was a constraint.

At the beginning of this year, I tried it again. Only this time, I assumed that the announcement of a program on spiritual gifts would not motivate the entire congregation to attend. I also assumed that those motivated by the topic would have greatly diverse expectations for the outcome of such a program. I began by getting the congregation involved in a simple focused activity. I did this where I had a captive audience for the greatest percentage of the congregation–in the Sunday

morning worship hour. I preached a sermon series on spiritual gifts.
Each week the sermon contained a tiny exercise aimed at getting the
congregation to participate in common means. One week members were
asked to recall the memory of a person who had influenced their lives. I
related the memory of the person to the use of spiritual gifts. Another
week I asked people to choose one of three types of potential motiva-
tions for helping others after the hurricane disaster in South Florida.
"Would you be more likely to become involved because of the devastat-
ing conditions of the victims, because of your altruistic nature, or because helping others would please God?" This question forced them to
ponder whether they might have one of the gifts of mercy, helping, or
service. For the final two weeks, I asked them to take notes regarding
various gifts and jot down certain items. Taking notes is actually one
form of common means.

At the end of the five-week sermon series, those wishing to complete a survey of their spiritual gifts were asked to remain in the sanctu-
ary rather than attend Sunday school. This time, more than eighty people
completed the survey, compared to twenty the previous time. Eighty
was still less than half the congregation, but it was four times as many as
participated in the last spiritual gifts emphasis.

I began the entire project by assuming diverse ends and tried to
involve as many as I could in common means. In the weeks that fol-
lowed, it was interesting to listen to common ends emerge. I heard comments such as, "Now that I have taken the survey, I can really begin to
see the benefit." Also, since the survey, I have begun to promote the
final component of the strategy—diverse means. I have continued to
explore with the congregation and individual members other means of
discovering spiritual gifts, such as prayer, discussions with friends and
family, and other resources.

Future Application

Most churches have no shortage of programs. As more and more people
have adopted a consumer mentality when "shopping" for a church,
churches have responded by adding more and better programs. Are the
programs making a difference? From my personal observation, many
people join a church because it offers a wide variety of programs, but
their participation is minimal. I may choose to buy a camcorder or

microwave oven with the most options but then only use one-tenth of the available functions.

Churches need to offer programs that make a difference in people's lives, not just attract large numbers. Certain types of programs may serve as motivating factors. The sheer announcement of softball teams, volleyball leagues, carry-in dinners, and video showings will often motivate people to join those particular activities. But many other very worthwhile programs operate as constraints rather than motivating factors for congregations. Churches need to find a way to get more people involved in the programs that are making a difference in people's lives. Adopting the means and ends strategy detailed above is one way to do this.

Warren Bennis suggests, "The intellectual life is really the ability to see how things can be different."[2] It is time for the church to use its intellectual capacity in designing new ways to do the will of God. God's basic instructions for the church have not changed. For centuries God has called the church to evangelize, disciple, and meet the needs of people. The duties of the church have not been altered. The means of accomplishing its duties, however, must be changed. What worked a hundred years ago is not working today. What works today may not work tomorrow. The church must constantly adjust its methods to accomplish its mission. It is time for the church to discover new ways of accomplishing traditional tasks. It is time for the church to learn to lead in a new way.

Using This Chapter with a Small Group

1.   Choose an existing activity or program within your church, one that you see as worthwhile but that people have not supported.

2.   How might you redesign the program by first recognizing the diverse ends that exist and promoting a common means activity?

3.   Continue to focus on this activity by brainstorming several possible diverse means that would expand it. Then analyze the variety of diverse ends people might associate with the activity.

4.   Develop your ideas into a plan of action and discuss the strategy with the individual or group in charge of the particular program.

5.   As an additional exercise, choose a mark of congregational maturity, such as spiritual formation, evangelism, or new member assimilation, in which you feel your congregation is particularly weak. Devise a way to get people more involved in this activity through the recognition of diverse ends, the promotion of common means, a recognition of common ends, an emphasis on diverse means, and a discussion of diverse ends.

NOTES

Chapter 1

1. Jude P. Dougherty, "What Was Religion? The Demise of a Prodigious Power," *Modern Age* 33, no. 2 (Summer 1990): 113.
2. Karl Weick, *The Social Psychology of Organizing* (Reading, Mass.: Addison-Wesley, 1979), 36.

Chapter 2

1. Karl Weick, *The Social Psychology of Organizing* (Reading, Mass.: Addison-Wesley, 1979), 72.
2. L. P. Gerlach and V. H. Hine, *People, Power, Change: Movements of Social Transformation* (New York: Bobbs-Merrill, 1970), 370-77.

Chapter 3

1. Chester Finn, "As Much Time as Necessary," *College Board Review* 161 (Fall 1991): 24-29.
2. Jean A. King, "Can We Achieve Outcome-Based Education?" *Educational Leadership* 49, no. 2 (October 1991): 73-75.
3. George N. Schmidt, "Chicago Mastery Reading: A Case against a Skills-Based Reading Curriculum," *Learning* 11, no. 4 (November 1982): 39-40.
4. Winston Marsh, "Working Smarter, Not Harder," *CPA Journal* 60, no. 3 (March 1990): 57.
5. Bill M. Sullivan, *Ten Steps to Breaking the 200 Barrier* (Kansas City, Mo.: Beacon Hill Press, 1988), 60.

6. Philipp Spener, *Pia Desideria*, trans. Theodore G. Tappert (Philadelphia: Fortress Press, 1964).

7. Howard A. Snyder, *Signs of the Spirit* (Grand Rapids: Zondervan, 1989), 38.

8. Kennon L. Callahan, *Effective Church Leadership* (San Francisco: Harper & Row, 1990), 209.

Chapter 4

1. Roy M. Oswald and Otto Kroeger, *Personality Type and Religious Leadership* (Washington, D.C.: The Alban Institute, 1988).

2. Gary L. Harbaugh, *God's Gifted People* (Minneapolis: Augsburg, 1990).

3. Lloyd Edwards, *How We Belong, Fight, and Pray: The MBTI as a Key to Congregational Dynamics* (Washington, D.C.: The Alban Institute, 1993), 18.

4. Ibid, 54.

5. William Bridges, *The Character of Organizations* (Palo Alto, Calif.: Consulting Psychologists Press, 1992).

6. Warren Bennis, *On Becoming a Leader* (Reading, Mass.: Addison-Wesley, 1989), 68.

Chapter 5

1. Thomas Peters and Robert Waterman, *In Search of Excellence: Lessons from America's Best Run Companies* (New York: Harper & Row, 1982), 318.

2. Karl Weick, "Educational Organizations as Loosely Coupled Systems," *Administrative Science Quarterly* 21 (1976): 1-19.

3. Terry Astuto and David Clark, "A Proposed Taxonomy of Organizational Coupling." (Mimeographed paper written for "organizational Theory," taught by David Clark, Indiana University, Fall 1985).

Chapter 6

1. David Halliday and Robert Resnick, *Physics: Parts I & II* (New York: John Wiley, 1960), 1177.

2. Max Plank, *The Universe in the Light of Modern Physics*, trans. W. H. Johnston (London: George Allen & Unwin, 1931), 8.

3. Daniel Liderbach, *The Numinous Universe* (Mahwah, N.J.: Paulist Press, 1989), 76.

4. Ibid., 85.

5. Ibid.

6. Ann and Barry Ulanov, *The Healing Imagination* (Mahwah, N.J.: Paulist Press, 1991), 32.

7. Norman Perrin, *Jesus and the Language of the Kingdom* (Philadelphia: Fortress Press, 1976), 33.

8. Liderbach, *The Numinous Universe*, 110.

9. Ibid., 111.

10. Morton Kelsey, *Encounter with God* (Mahwah, N.J.: Paulist Press, 1972), 36.

11. Loren Mead, *The Once and Future Church* (Washington D.C.: The Alban Institute, 1991), 6.

12. Ibid., 25.

13. Kennon Callahan, *Effective Church Leadership* (San Francisco: Harper & Row, 1990), 13.

Chapter 7

1. Herbert A. Simon, "On the Concept of Organizational Goal," *Administrative Science Quarterly* 9, no. 1 (June 1964): 1-22.

2. Ibid., 20.

3. Ibid., 8.

4. William Bryan Quinn, *Strategies for Change: Logical Incrementalism* (Homewood, Ill.: Richard D. Irwin, Inc., 1980).

Chapter 8

1. James D. Glasse, *Putting It Together in the Parish* (Nashville: Abingdon Press, 1972), 21.

2. Charles Perrow, "Disintegrating Social Sciences," *Phi Delta Kappan* 63, no. 10 (June 1982): 684-88.

3. Ibid., 685.

4. B. F. Skinner, "The Phylogeny and Ontogeny of Behavior," *Science* 153 (1966): 1205-13.

5. H. Garfinkel, "Common-Sense Knowledge of Social Structures:

The Documentary Method of Interpretation." In *Theories of the Mind*, ed. J. Scher (New York: Free Press, 1962), 689-712.

6. D. J. Bem, "Self-Perception: The Dependent Variable of Human Performance," *Organizational Behavior and Human Performance* 2 (1967): 105-21.

7. Warren Bennis, *On Becoming a Leader* (Reading, Mass.: Addison-Wesley, 1990), 116.

8. Perrow, "Disintegrating Social Sciences," 685.

9. Kennon Callahan, *Effective Church Leadership* (San Francisco: Harper & Row, 1990), 203.

Chapter 9

1. James D. Glasse, *Putting It Together in the Parish* (Nashville: Abingdon Press, 1972), 108.

2. Kenneth C. Haugk, *Antagonists in the Church* (Minneapolis: Augsburg, 1988), 21-22.

Chapter 10

1. Karl Weick, *The Social Psychology of Organizing* (Reading, Mass.: Addison-Wesley, 1979), 91.

2. Warren Bennis, *On Becoming a Leader* (Reading, Mass.: Addison-Wesley, 1989), 85.

BIBLIOGRAPHY

Astuto, Terry, and David Clark. "A Proposed Taxonomy of Organizational Coupling" (Mimeographed paper written for "Organizational Theory," taught by David Clark, Indiana University, Fall 1985).

Bem, D. J. "Self-Perception: The Dependent Variable of Human Performance." *Organizational Behavior and Human Performance* 2 (1967): 105-121.

Bennis, Warren. *On Becoming a Leader*. Reading, Mass.: Addison-Wesley, 1989.

Bridges, William. *The Character of Organizations*. Palo Alto, Calif.: Consulting Psychologists Press, 1992.

Callahan, Kennon. *Effective Church Leadership*. San Francisco: Harper & Row, 1990.

Dougherty, Jude P. "What Was Religion: The Demise of a Prodigious Power." *Modern Age* 33, no. 2 (Summer 1990): 113.

Edwards, Lloyd. *How We Belong, Fight, and Pray: The MBTI as a Key to Congregational Dynamics*. Washington, D.C.: The Alban Institute, 1993.

Finn, Chester. "As Much Time as Necessary." *College Board Review* 161 (Fall 1991): 24-29.

Garfinkel, H. "Common-Sense Knowledge of Social Structures: The Documentary Method of Interpretation." In *Theories of the Mind*, edited by J. Scher. New York: Free Press, 1962.

Gerlach, L. P., and V. H. Hine. *People, Power, Change: Movements of Social Transformation*. New York: Bobbs-Merrill, 1970.

Glasse, James D. *Putting It Together in the Parish*. Nashville: Abingdon Press, 1972.

Halliday, David, and Robert Resnick. *Physics: Parts I & II*. New York: John Wiley, 1960.

Harbaugh, Gary L. *God's Gifted People*. Minneapolis: Augsburg, 1990.

Haugk, Kenneth C. *Antagonists in the Church*. Minneapolis: Augsburg, 1988.

Kelsey, Morton. *Encounter with God*. Mahwah, N.J.: Paulist Press, 1972.

King, Jean A. "Can We Achieve Outcome-Based Education?" *Educational Leadership* 49, no. 2 (October 1991): 73-75.

Liderbach, Daniel. *The Numinous Universe*. Mahwah, N.J.: Paulist Press, 1989.

Marsh, Winston. "Working Smarter, Not Harder." *CPA Journal* 60, no. 3 (March 1990): 57.

Mead, Loren. *The Once and Future Church*. Washington, D.C.: The Alban Institute, 1991.

Olsen, Charles M. "Research: What Makes Church Boards Work? Part I: Why Do Church Board Members Burn Out?" *Congregations* (May-June 1993): 10-12.

Olsen, Charles M. "Research: What Makes Church Boards Work? Part II: Church Boards as Spiritual Leaders." *Congregations* (July-August 1993): 16-18.

Oswald, Roy M., and Otto Kroeger. *Personality Type and Religious Leadership.* Washington, D.C.: Alban Institute, 1988.

Perrin, Norman. *Jesus and the Language of the Kingdom.* Philadelphia: Fortress Press, 1976.

Perrow, Charles. "Disintegrating Social Sciences." *Phi Delta Kappan* 63, no. 10 (June 1982): 684-88.

Peters, Thomas, and Robert Waterman. I*n Search of Excellence: Lessons from America's Best Run Companies.* New York: Harper & Row, 1982.

Plank, Max. *The Universe in the Light of Modern Physics.* Translated by W. H. Johnston. London: George Allen & Unwin, 1931.

Quinn, William Bryan. *Strategies for Change: Logical Incrementalism.* Homewood, Ill.: Richard D. Irwin, 1980.

Resnick, Robert, and David Halliday. *Basic Concepts in Relativity and Early Quantum Theory.* New York: Wiley, 1985.

Schmidt, George N. "Chicago Mastery Reading: A Case against a Skills-Based Reading Curriculum." *Learning* 11, no. 4 (November 1982): 39-40.

Simon, Herbert. "On the Concept of Organizational Goal." *Administrative Science Quarterly* 9, no. 1 (June 1964): 1-22.

Skinner, B. F. "The Phylogeny and Ontogeny of Behavior." *Science* 153 (1966): 1205-13.

Snyder, Howard A. *Signs of the Spirit.* Grand Rapids: Zondervan, 1989.

Spener, Philipp. *Pia Desideria.* Translated by Theodore G. Tappert. Philadelphia: Fortress Press, 1964.

Sullivan, Bill M. *Ten Steps to Breaking the 200 Barrier.* Kansas City, Mo.: Beacon Hill, 1988.

Ulanov, Ann, and Barry Ulanov. *The Healing Imagination.* Mahwah, N.J.: Paulist Press, 1991.

Weick, Karl. *The Social Psychology of Organizing.* Reading, Mass.: Addison-Wesley, 1979.

Weick, Karl. "Educational Organizations as Loosely Coupled Systems." *Administrative Science Quarterly* 21 (1976): 1-19.

Woods, C. Jeff. "Using Organizational Coupling as a Variable in Church Structure." *Sharing the Practice* (Spring 1987): 19-22.

Woods, C. Jeff. "A Long Range Planning Primer." *Clergy Journal* (March 1992): 20-22.

Woods, C. Jeff. "Surveying to Find a Church's Distinctiveness." *Christian Ministry* (January-February 1991): 11-14.